Lesley and Roy Adkins are authors of numerou
books, including *The Handbook of British Archaeology, Archaeological Illustration, Abandoned Places, An Introduction to Archaeology, Talking Archaeology,* and *Introduction to the Romans.* They are both archaeological consultants and are members of the Institute of Field Archaeologists. They live at Aller, near Langport, in Somerset.

Following page
The gatehouse of Cleeve Abbey

A Field Guide to
Somerset Archaeology

Lesley and Roy Adkins

THE DOVECOTE PRESS

This book is dedicated to
Lesley Falconer and Phil Edginton

First published in 1992 by The Dovecote Press Ltd
Stanbridge, Wimborne, Dorset BH21 4JD

ISBN 0 946159 94 7

Designed by Humphrey Stone
Photoset in Palatino by The Typesetting Bureau,
Wimborne, Dorset
Printed and bound in Singapore

Contents

Acknowledgements

We would like to thank the following people and organisations for their assistance: the curators and staff of the various monuments, museums and information centres visited by us; Stephen Minnitt, Bob Croft and Russell Lillford for reading and commenting on the text; David Bromwich and Elizabeth Clark for their invaluable help in the local history library; Royal Commission on the Historical Monuments of England (Exeter), in particular Paul Pattison, Ian Sainsbury and Christopher Dunn, for information on several sites; Chris Webster for smoothing our way through the county's SMR; Bruce Watkin and Mrs J. M. Rainer for assisting us in the Somerset Archaeological and Natural History Society's library; Mick Aston for provision of photographs; and those landowners and tenants who provided well-maintained footpaths, stiles and gates.

CONVERSION TABLE	
1 centimetre	0·4 inches
10 centimetres	3·9 inches
20 centimetres	7·9 inches
50 centimetres	1 foot 8 inches
1 metre	1 yard 4 inches
10 metres	10 yards 2 feet 8 inches
50 metres	54 yards 2 feet 1 inch
1 kilometre	5/8 mile
1 hectare	2·48 acres
1 square kilometre	248 acres or 0·39 square mile

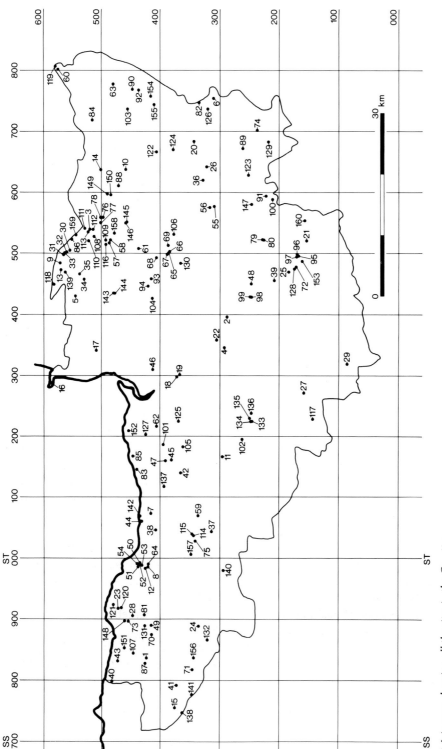

Main map showing all the sites in the Gazetteer

Introduction

This book is for anyone, whatever their level of archaeological and historical knowledge, who is interested in Somerset's past. Its primary aim is to help the reader find and understand the visible sites, and to point the way to further sources of information for those who wish to study them in greater detail.

Archaeological sites dating from the Palaeolithic period to the end of the Medieval period are included, but to keep the book to a manageable length, Post-Medieval (including industrial archaeology) sites have been excluded, as have most churches and other standing buildings. Only a selection of some particular sites has been included, such as crosses, round barrows, and Medieval field systems. Sites no longer visible to the visitor are largely excluded, as are inaccessible sites on private land (even if they were included in previous guidebooks). However, those sites on private land that can be clearly seen from a public right of way are included, as well as ones open to the public in the care of bodies such as English Heritage and the National Trust. Even areas such as Exmoor are mainly privately owned, and public access is only possible along rights of way.

Regrettably in these days of fast-moving road traffic, it is rarely possible to dawdle along a busy through-route trying to pinpoint a particular site. We have therefore tried to give as much information as possible to make it easier to locate sites quickly.

Some sites in this field guide may not be visible when crops and grassland are at peak growth. On the other hand, visitors may recognise more sites than those mentioned here, particularly sites with more ephemeral remains; with experience, many features of the landscape can be discerned, such as traces of earthworks representing former Medieval villages.

The local government changes of 1974 lopped off the north-east corner of the historic county of Somerset, which is now incorporated in Avon. The new county boundary has been used in this book, and so only sites within the present county boundary have been included.

How to Use this Field Guide

The guide has three main sections: this Introduction, a short general introduction to the archaeology of the county, and the Gazetteer of the sites in alphabetical order. There are also lists and tables which provide a quick reference for various types of information. A good starting point is to look at the main map, choose a site that is near where you are or where you are going, and look that up in the Gazetteer. Each Gazetteer entry ends with a reference to the nearest sites to enable a route to be plotted.

Included in the Gazetteer entries are road directions, national grid references (some SS, but mostly ST), car parking, facilities (such as toilets and refreshments), opening times (where applicable), and a description of the site.

A reading list is given for those people who wish to research a site in greater depth. This is given as, for example, 'Grinsell 1971', the full

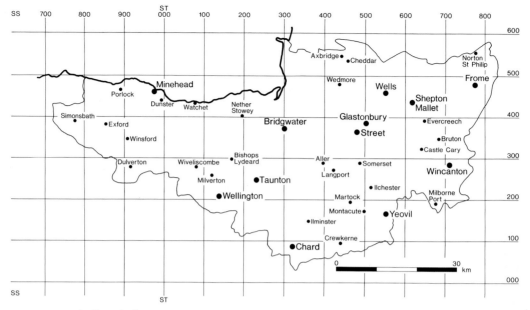

Main towns and villages in Somerset.

reference for which is in the bibliography at the end of the book.

Access or partial access for people with a disability is stated as fully as possible to help them assess in advance whether they will be able to visit a site. Estimates of accessibility have been based on the assumption that the disabled person is in a wheelchair and has the assistance of a companion.

All measurements in the text are given using the metric system, but a conversion table of metric to imperial units is given on p.7.

Rights of Way

Naturally, visitors should abide by the Countryside Code, in particular by keeping to footpaths and by shutting all gates (even open ones). Unfortunately, similar thought is not always given to the visitor, as public rights of way in Somerset are in a mixed condition, with a lack of stiles, gates often being difficult to open, and gates held shut by fraying baler twine and even barbed wire. Footpaths are only occasionally signposted or waymarked, and some are blocked by barbed wire, padlocked gates and other obstructions. Any problems, particularly obstructions such as barbed wire and ploughed-up paths, should be explained to the appropriate authority (preferably with a photocopy of a relevant map or a sketch) so that the situation can be improved. A list of addresses of authorities can be found towards the end of the book. If you are unsure of the area in which the footpath is situated, the County Council should be contacted, so that the problem can be forwarded to the correct authority.

The best maps to use are the Ordnance Survey 1:25000 Pathfinder series which give a reasonable amount of detail and show rights of way. A set of twenty-eight maps is needed to cover the entire county of Somerset. In places such as Exmoor, where the weather is unpredictable, and visibility can be suddenly restricted by rain or fog, it is advisable to take maps and a compass, and not rely solely on the directions given in this field guide.

Travelling to Sites

It is assumed that most visitors will travel by car or by coach. Parking can sometimes be difficult, particularly in narrow lanes, and great care should be taken not to cause an obstruction or block access to field gates. Visitors are advised to use well-frequented car parks wherever possible, lock their cars and not leave valuables on display in their vehicles, because thieves often target isolated car parks.

Public transport is not in great abundance, but details can be obtained from libraries and tourist information centres. The only British Rail stations in the whole of Somerset are at Frome, Templecombe, Taunton, Bridgwater, Castle Cary, Highbridge, Crewkerne and Bruton, and two stations at Yeovil. There are also two private steam lines (East and West Somerset).

Museums

Finds from excavated sites in Somerset have over the decades been deposited in a number of museums, most notably the County Museum in Taunton, King John's Hunting Lodge in Axbridge, the Admiral Blake Museum in Bridgwater, Wells Museum, Cheddar Caves Museum, the Bristol City Museum and Art Gallery, and the Bristol Spelaeological Society Museum. Finds have also been deposited in museums farther afield such as the British Museum, the British Museum (Natural History), and museums in Oxford, Manchester and Cambridge. Many finds in these museums are not on display but are held in store for study by researchers. Other finds, particularly those from older excavations, have been lost, destroyed or remain in private ownership.

Only well-run museums in Somerset which contain archaeological collections of a reasonable size have been included in this field guide: those with unreliable opening times have been excluded.

Geology and Relief

The geology of Somerset is reflected in its landscape, which has an extensive low-lying area (the Somerset Levels), open to the Bristol Channel on the north-west and hemmed in by hills on the other sides. The central area of the Levels consists of alluvial and peat deposits, and has been subject to marine and fresh water flooding throughout its history. Attempts at drainage and flood defences began in the Roman period, if not earlier, and the struggle to control flooding in the Levels has continued to this day.

To the south and east of the Levels, areas of clay and limestone form rising land, while to the north-east the area is bounded by the limestone and sandstone plateau of the Mendips. To the west the land rises more steeply to the sandstone moorland of Exmoor (most of which is in Somerset), the Quantocks and the Brendon Hills, and to the south-west the Blackdown Hills.

The River Parrett bisects the county and also marks a difference in nature between the eastern and western halves. In the north-east, the Mendip Hills and the River Avon (outside the county) form substantial natural barriers, but there are few serious obstacles to travel in the east and south. This latter area is generally suitable for settlement, with a variety of soil types providing both pasture and arable land. For the early hunter-gatherers, travelling through rather than settling in the area, the diversity of soils provided equally diverse natural vegetation, while the limestone caves of the Mendips offered temporary shelter.

By contrast, much of the land to the west of the River Parrett is characterised by the underlying sandstones. The soils are often thin, and the land rises steeply in the west to the more inhospitable areas of Exmoor. Consequently, settlements in this area are smaller and more scattered than in the eastern half of the county, and up until the nineteenth century large areas of these western uplands were

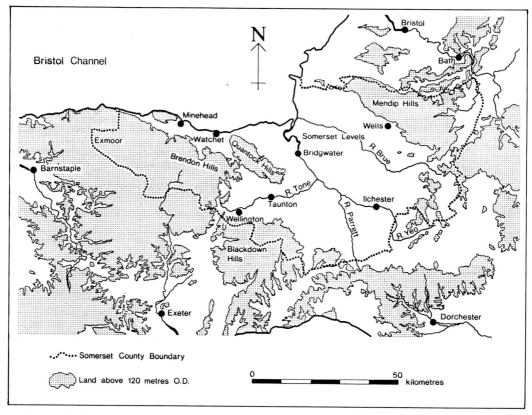

N

Bristol Channel

Bristol

Bath

Mendip Hills

Wells

Minehead

Exmoor

Watchet

Somerset Levels

R Brue

Brendon Hills

Quantock Hills

Bridgwater

Barnstaple

R Tone

Ilchester

Taunton

R Parrett

R Yeo

Wellington

Blackdown Hills

Exeter

Dorchester

····ꞏ···· Somerset County Boundary

Land above 120 metres O.D.

0   50
kilometres

High ground and rivers in the Somerset region.

uninhabited.

The county covers the boundary between the Lowland and Highland Zones of Britain. The Lowland Zone to the east is an area with an hospitable landscape and good agricultural soil that are conducive to settlement, while in the Highland Zone to the west, the landscape, soil and climate make agriculture very difficult. As a result, Somerset has often been something of a border territory. For example, during the Roman period, much of Somerset was intensively settled, with farming establishments centred around Ilchester. Yet the Roman occupation in the extreme west of Somerset and beyond was nowhere near as intense, and in many places was little more than a military frontier zone. The nature of the Somerset landscape determined that this area was the most westerly area of effective Romanisation.

The landscape also had an influence on settlement through the location of mineral and building stone deposits. Lead and silver in the Mendip Hills were mined in the Iron Age and were extensively exploited during the Roman period, while iron was mined in the Brendon Hills, and stone was quarried from various sources across the county.

Threatened Sites

Archaeological sites (even those protected by legislation) are being constantly damaged and destroyed, often with little or no record, through development of town and countryside and farming practices. Many of

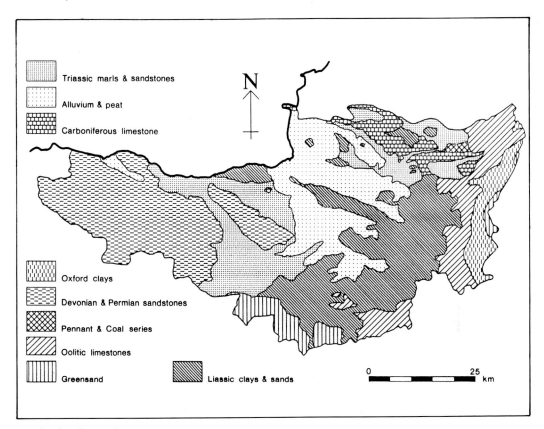

 Inside the map:

Triassic marls & sandstones

Alluvium & peat

Carboniferous limestone

N

Oxford clays

Devonian & Permian sandstones

Pennant & Coal series

Oolitic limestones

Greensand

Liassic clays & sands

0   25
         km

Simplified geology of the county of Somerset.

the sites mentioned in this guidebook are Scheduled Ancient Monuments, and it is an offence to interfere with any such monument, such as by digging or by using a metal detector, without the written permission of the Secretary of State for the Environment. It should not be assumed that all sites have been recorded, and people wishing to participate in much-needed non-destructive recording of sites should contact their local archaeological society or join some of the more practical evening classes and day-schools (details are held in libraries).

Even a site which is recorded before its destruction is little consolation for those who want to visit sites. In particular, numerous Medieval deserted village earthworks and field systems are being inexorably ploughed

flat. For example, in 1979 the deserted village at Vallis near Frome was bulldozed and filled in, in 1976 a deserted village was bulldozed and flattened at Odcombe, and Aston (1988b, 85) noted that many areas of ridge-and-furrow which showed on RAF aerial photographs of the 1940s have now been ploughed flat. After surviving for centuries, or even for millennia, much of the prehistoric and historic landscape is under threat. Visitors should be aware that what they see around them today may be gone tomorrow. A legend states that if the Wick Barrow is removed by day, it will be replaced during the night (Grinsell 1976, 104): would that the legend were true for all the sites in the county.

The Archaeological Periods

Palaeolithic, before 70,000 BC – 8300 BC

Only a small number of Palaeolithic sites is known in the county. For the Lower Palaeolithic, a handful of sites and stone tools (including handaxes) has been recorded, although a cave site at Westbury-sub-Mendip has recently produced evidence for human activity possibly dating back half a million years. This cave site was found in 1969 during limestone quarrying operations, and humanly struck flint was found which appeared to be associated with Middle Pleistocene deposits of the late Cromerian interglacial. Similarly, the Middle Palaeolithic has yielded very little evidence in Somerset, although one cave site at Wookey Hole (the Hyaena Den) is known to have been occupied during this period.

It is mainly the Mendip region which has produced evidence of human activity before 18,000 BC. After then, the severity of the glacial climate prevented occupation for a long period. It was only towards the end of the last glaciation that the area was occupied once again (around 12,000-9000 BC), by which time modern man (Homo sapiens sapiens) had reached Britain. Several caves and shelters in the Mendip area of Somerset and Avon have produced evidence of use at this time (Upper Palaeolithic), in particular those in Cheddar Gorge and at Wookey Hole. The contemporary landscape would have been mainly tundra and heath, with a small amount of willow and birch woodland, and the animals hunted would have included horse, red deer and reindeer. By about 9000 BC the tundra-like conditions were giving way to deciduous woodland as the climate improved and the Ice Age came to an end. The Ice Age hunters adapted their way of life to one of less specialised hunting and gathering, and the ensuing period is termed the Mesolithic.

Mesolithic, 8300 BC – 4000BC

The end of the last Ice Age was around 8300 BC, and the resulting improvement in climate led to the development of increased forest and the rising of the sea level, which caused the separation of Britain from the Continent by the English Channel. The Mesolithic sites and finds span a period of some 4000 years. Scattered finds of worked flint and chert have been discovered across the county, but sites and finds are known mainly from the north and west of the county, including coastal areas around Watchet, the Somerset Levels around Middlezoy and Shapwick, Exmoor, and the Mendips. At the end of the Ice Age, the Somerset Levels probably comprised a series of broad river valleys separated by low ridges which were sometimes capped by marine sand deposits (Burtle Beds). During the 7th millenium BC the sea level rose, the Levels were covered by the sea for the next 2000 years, and adjacent areas were waterlogged. A burial, known as 'Cheddar Man', which was found in Gough's Cave, has been dated to this period.

Neolithic, 4000 BC – 2300 BC

The Neolithic spans some 2000 years dating from around 4000 BC. Evidence for Neolithic sites in Somerset is relatively scarce, although excavations over the years have helped to fill some gaps in the record. For instance, pits, hearths and artefacts have been found at South Cadbury dating to the early 3rd millenium BC. Neolithic levels of occupation, including pottery and flint artefacts, have also been found in several Mendip caves and rock shelters, such as Chelm's Combe and Tom Tivey's Hole, and some caves were also used for human burials in the Neolithic period. Finds of flint and stone artefacts, including axeheads, have been found across the county, indicating widespread activity at this time, and numerous such finds have been discovered at Ham Hill. Flint would have been brought into the county (probably from Wiltshire), as none occurs naturally in Somerset, although small deposits of chert do occur. The stone axes have been shown to originate from much further afield, including Cornwall.

Long barrows (mounds) were often used for the burial of the dead in the Neolithic period, and several long barrows are known in the old county (now part of Avon). From modern-day Somerset only a few dubious examples of long barrows are known, including the possible burial chamber at Battlegore, Williton. Situated fairly close to the Avon/Somerset border, and therefore near the Avon long barrows, are the Priddy Circles. These are a row of four henge monuments, probably later Neolithic in date, and are extremely important monuments for Britain. Unfortunately they are barely visible on the ground, although they can be clearly seen from the air. Only three kilometres to the east is a smaller henge monument, Gorsey Bigbury, but it is not accessible to visitors.

By far the majority of evidence for the Neolithic in Somerset has come from the work undertaken in recent years in the Levels (Peat Moors) to the north of the Polden Hills. During the Mesolithic, the Levels were an inlet of the sea, and marine clays and silts were deposited, but by 4500 BC the area had become an estuarine swamp, and peat and woodland developed. The peat continued to develop, up to ten metres thick in places, until about AD 400 when climatic conditions halted its formation. Amongst the many finds excavated from the waterlogged deposits have been extensive wooden trackways which originally linked the hills with the various islands. The evidence for activity in the Levels suggests that there are extensive Neolithic settlements on higher ground nearby that await discovery.

Bronze Age, 2300 BC – 700 BC

Towards the end of the Neolithic and the beginning of the Bronze Age, Beaker pottery was in use, examples of which have been found across the county. Some Beaker pottery has also been found in human burials, mainly under round barrows (such as Wick Barrow), within stone-lined cists, and in cave deposits in the Mendips. From around 2300-1400 BC (Early Bronze Age), round barrows (often referred to on maps as 'tumuli') were the main class of monument for the burial of the dead. Numerous round barrows are known across the county, and many are still visible. A large number of them were inadequately excavated in the 19th century, mainly by the Rev. John Skinner, and collared urns were found to be frequently deposited with the burials. The main concentrations of round barrows are in the Mendips, Exmoor, Brendon Hills and the Quantocks, but numerous Early Bronze Age finds (such as bronze artefacts and stone axe-hammers) have also been discovered across the county, and the henge monuments of the Priddy Circles and Gorsey Bigbury were probably still in use at this time.

The period from 1400-1000 BC (Middle Bronze Age) is characterised in Somerset by several important groups of bronze artefacts which have given the term 'Taunton phase' to this period of metalworking in Britain. The metalwork has been found mainly in river valleys, but not a great deal is known about associated settlements. Contemporary pottery (called 'Deverel-Rimbury' pottery) has been recorded in Somerset, and a few sites of this date have been excavated, including a large enclosure at Norton Fitzwarren which pre-dated the Iron Age hillfort. In the Somerset Levels, from 2000-1000 BC, a large number of trackways existed across the wet moorlands, and so there are likely to have been settle-ments nearby.

The Late Bronze Age from around 1000-700 BC sees a development in bronzework, ex-amples of which have been found throughout the county, again mainly from river valleys. A few domestic sites are known from excava-tions including hilltop sites such as South Cad-bury and Norton Fitzwarren.

Iron Age, 700 BC — AD 43

The Iron Age extended from the 6th century BC to the mid 1st century AD (Roman invasion). From the 6th-4th centuries BC there is evidence that hilltop sites such as South Cadbury, Brean Down and Ham Hill were occupied. There is no evidence that the latter site was defended at this time, but South Cadbury was fortified by a rampart. Some of the Mendip caves, such as Gough's Cave, were also used at this period. Little is known about early Iron Age settlement in west Somerset, although Norton Fitzwarren con-tinued to be occupied as a hillfort, and other hillforts were constructed for the first time.

The period from the 4th-1st centuries BC sees the appearance of a new distinctive type of pottery, which has been termed 'Glaston-bury' ware. Some early hillforts went out of use, while others continued to be occupied and strengthened (such as South Cadbury and Ham Hill), following the pattern seen further

east in Wessex. Hillforts occur over most areas of Somerset, except for the higher parts of Exmoor and Mendip and in the Somerset Levels; west of the River Parrett the hillforts are much smaller but more numerous. Little is known of non-hillfort settlements of this date, except for the two major settlements in the Somerset Levels: Glastonbury and Meare. Many Mendip caves also continued to be used for domestic occupation.

During the 1st century BC to 1st century AD many hillforts elsewhere were abandoned, and large lowland settlements known as 'op-pida' developed. The situation is likely to have been similar in Somerset. During the 1st century BC the county was probably divided between three tribes. The western part was probably the territory of the Dumnonii, while the east of the county was divided between the Dobunni in the north and the Durotriges in the south, with a possible boundary along the Brue valley.

Roman Period, AD 43 — 410

The Roman conquest of Britain took place in AD 43, and by AD 49 the Fosse Way had been constructed as a military road connecting a series of forts. Forts existed at Ilchester and possibly at Shepton Mallet, and forts are also believed to have existed beyond the Fosse Way at Ham Hill, South Cadbury, Char-terhouse and Wiveliscombe. A great deal is known about civilian settlement in Somer-set in the Roman period, and much of the landscape was densely populated apart from some areas of forest, parts of the Levels, and the higher areas of Exmoor and the Quan-tocks. Numerous villas are known, which were established from the 1st century AD onwards. Some hillfort sites continued to be used in the Roman period, at times for religious purposes, and there were also other farmsteads and large settlements. The town of Ilchester was prob-ably the most important centre in Roman

Somerset. Being in the middle of a fertile valley, it was surrounded by numerous villas, many of which displayed a high degree of prosperity. There were also other large settlements, such as an extensive roadside settlement at Shepton Mallet along the Fosse Way. The Fosse Way was the principal road, and the Ilchester to Dorchester road was also important. River and sea transport was used as well, and possible ports are known along the River Parrett.

Large-scale industry was introduced from an early date, and included the extensive mining of silver and lead around Charterhouse on the Mendips, pottery manufacture at Shepton Mallet, and salt production on the Levels. By the end of the 1st century AD, the coastal marshes were being drained and coastal flood defences were being constructed.

Despite the large body of evidence for the Roman period in Somerset, there are virtually no visible remains for people to visit, and the Roman period therefore seems (incorrectly) a blank period in the county.

By the end of the Roman period in the early 5th century, many settlements were abandoned, but others continued in use into the Saxon and Medieval periods.

Saxon Period, AD 410 – 1066

The earlier part of this period (410-700) is usually described as the Dark Ages, but from 700 the area came under Saxon domination. Roman military forces and administration were withdrawn from Britain in the early 5th century, and this early period of history is linked in Somerset with the legendary King Arthur. The use of Latin gave way to the Celtic language, and many Roman sites such as villas and small settlements were abandoned. Insufficient is known in Somerset about early Dark Age settlements, but some hilltop sites, such as South Cadbury and Glastonbury Tor were certainly occupied.

During the 7th century the Saxons advanced into Somerset, which from the 8th century became one of the shires of the West Saxon kingdom. Saxon kings are known to have visited various places such as Glastonbury, Frome and Cheddar, and excavations at the latter site have yielded information on the type of royal residence which existed at that period. In the mid 9th century there were Danish invasions in Somerset, but the Danes were eventually defeated by King Alfred. Numerous charters detailing estate boundaries and also other written sources exist for the period 700-1066, and these are an important source of information.

The Christian church is known at an early date in Saxon Somerset, although there are few visible remains. Important early Christian foundations existed at places such as Muchelney, Glastonbury and Wells.

From early in this period there are likely to have been small villages and fortified centres, and from the 10th century there were fortified sites known as 'burhs' from the evidence of the document known as the 'Burghal Hidage'. This lists burhs for Somerset at Bath (now in Avon), Watchet, Axbridge, Lyng and Langport. These burhs were intended as protection against Danish invasions from the sea. Lyng appears to have been a fort while the others were small towns, all apparently fortified by walls. By the late 10th century Lyng came to be abandoned, while additional towns and mints for coins (such as Taunton, Ilchester and Bruton) appear in documentary sources, so that by the Norman Conquest Somerset had a well-developed system of towns.

Medieval, 1066 – 1550

Much more is known of the period from the Norman Conquest to the Dissolution of the Monasteries (1066 to c. 1540), because many of the settlements, buildings, field patterns and other features remain today, and much documentary evidence has also survived. Towns continued to develop, although some witnessed a shift in position from their Saxon town centres. Several new planned towns were also established, some of which have since disappeared or have been reduced to very small settlements, such as Merryfield (established as a borough by 1275 in the parish of East Coker), Newport ('new market') in North Curry (probably founded at the end of the 12th century) and Stoford near Yeovil (which had been founded before 1273 when it had a population of more than 500). Some new towns were founded by expanding existing villages such as at Bridgwater, Shepton Mallet and Montacute.

In the Medieval period there were also numerous villages, hamlets and farms. A number of these sites eventually became deserted or considerably reduced in size, but villages which have totally disappeared are rare in Somerset — usually churches, farms and cottages survive. Earthworks often exist (although many more have been ploughed flat in recent decades) indicating the previous existence of buildings and roads. Most of these deserted sites are situated in the south and east of the county, but it now seems that few villages were depopulated as a direct effect of the Black Death. Some became deserted from the 15th century following enclosure of the land for sheep farming and emparking, while others became deserted due to economic changes. In west Somerset and in areas such as Mendip, villages are few, but many Medieval farmsteads and small hamlets are also known to have been eventually deserted in these areas.

One of the most prominent types of Medieval site is the castle, several of which survive in Somerset, the two earliest being at Dunster and Montacute, which are both mentioned in the Domesday Book of 1086. Many of the earlier castles consisted of a motte (mound) with a timber or stone-built keep (tower) on top. The motte was sometimes artificial or else a natural hill was used. Later on one or more baileys (enclosures) were added at the base of the motte to protect further buildings. In most cases, only the motte and sometimes the bailey earthworks survive, with little or no evidence for the buildings. Subsequently, castles with stone walls and keeps were built, at places such as Taunton, Nunney and Farleigh Hungerford.

The other prominent type of Medieval site was the monastery, which varied in size from numerous small houses to the very important site at Glastonbury. The main Benedictine abbeys were at Glastonbury, Muchelney and Athelney, while a Cluniac priory existed at Montacute, and a Cistercian monastery at Cleeve. The most austere order was the Carthusian, of which Witham Charterhouse is an important example. There was also a large group of Augustinian houses such as at Taunton and Bruton, while at Wells there was a cathedral and bishop. The Church had an immense impact on the landscape, being by far the largest landowner in the county and a powerful economic force.

Other types of Medieval site are still visible in the landscape (although not always with public access) including moated sites, windmill mounds, church and chapel sites, and field systems. All over south-east Somerset in particular there are the visible remains of Medieval open fields in the form of ridge-and-furrow, with lynchets (terracing of the hillside) probably representing cultivation.

The Gazetteer

1 ALDERMAN'S BARROW (Bronze Age round barrow)

Location SS 836 423. Four kilometres north-west of Exford on Exmoor. Alderman's Barrow is signposted with a footpath sign from the Porlock-Exford road, and is situated on the southern side of the road from Lucott Cross to Wellshead, 250 metres north-east of the cattle grid. The barrow is marked by a metal post surmounted by a star.

Parking. There is room to park just before the cattle grid.

Access for disabled visitors. The barrow is situated on the roadside.

Site description. This is a large isolated Bronze Age round barrow, about 1.2 metres high and 27.4 metres across, but a covering of heather makes it appear rather shapeless. Like many others, this prehistoric barrow must have been a landmark for some 3000 years: it is now situated at the boundary of three parishes, and has probably been used to mark one of the bounds of Exmoor Forest since the 13th century. The barrow was used as a boundary mark in the perambulations of Exmoor Forest of 1219, 1298, 1301 and 1815, and was referred to as 'Osmundesburgh', with variations of this name from 1219 to 1301, and 'Owlaman's Burrow' from 1651 to 1815, with variants of the name after then.

Reading. Grinsell 1969, 8, 16, 19, 31.

Nearby sites. 70 Great Rowbarrow and Little Rowbarrow; 87 Madacombe; 107 Porlock Common; 151 Whit Stones.

2 ALLER (Saxon font, King Alfred's window)

Location ST 396 288. Three kilometres north-west of Langport, along the A372 road. Take the turning westwards by the Old Pound pub, and after 100 metres turn left, up the road signposted 'Ancient Church', to St. Andrew's Church. The font is in the south-west corner of the church, and the window is in the north wall of the chancel.

Parking. There is limited roadside parking.

Access for disabled visitors. Parking is possible outside the churchyard. There is one step into the churchyard and one step into the south porch of the church.

Facilities. Refreshments are available in the village.

Site description. The font which is in the south-west corner of the nave was retrieved from a pond in the vicarage garden around 1870. It is a simple limestone bowl-shaped font with an angular rim and skirt, resting on a modern shaft. The overall height is 0.87 metres. It is possibly of Saxon date and is one of only three Saxon fonts known in the modern county. Aller is first mentioned in the *Anglo-Saxon Chronicle*, where it is recorded that Guthrum, King of the Danes, came to the church at Aller and was baptised by Alfred, after being defeated by him. The Saxon font may have been the one in which Guthrum was baptised. The original Saxon settlement was probably in the vicinity of the church.

In the north wall of the chancel there is a stained glass window depicting King Alfred which was inserted in 1901. In the north-east corner of the north aisle there is an octagonal font dated 1663, which was obviously a replacement for the lost Saxon font.

Reading. Foster 1987, 68, 71.

Nearby sites. 4 Athelney Abbey; 22 Burrow Mump; 98, 99 Muchelney.

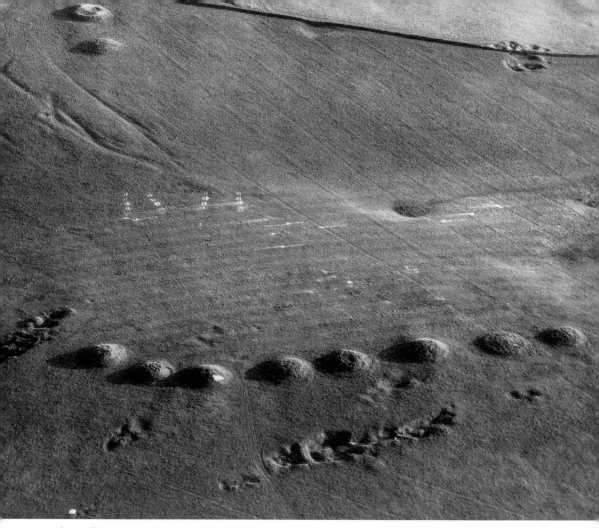

Ashen Hill Barrows, with two of the Priddy Nine Barrows in the top left hand corner (Cambridge University Collection: copyright reserved).

3 ASHEN HILL BARROWS, Priddy
(Bronze Age round barrows)

Location and parking ST 539 520. There is very limited verge parking on the north side of the B3135 road at ST 539 523, midway between Harptree Lodge and Cranmore View, and west of the Miners Arms Restaurant. On the south side of the road is a pair of field gates and a track through a narrow belt of woodland, from where the barrows can be seen on the skyline. The public footpath leads through the gates and across the pasture field to the barrows.

Alternatively, there is a little more room to park in Nine Barrows Lane (leading north-east from Priddy to the B3135 road at Bowery Corner) opposite a wide grass verge with trees. A public footpath leads through a small gate back to the other footpath at the double gates.

Access for disabled visitors. The barrows can be seen on the skyline from the field gates.

Site description. These are a spectacular group of eight Bronze Age round barrows, often confused with the nearby Priddy Nine Barrows (even on published maps). They used to be referred to as the Nine Barrows North group. At one time they were considered to be the Priddy Nine Barrows (and the Priddy Nine Barrows therefore the Ashen Hill barrows). However, Grinsell showed that the more southerly Priddy Nine Barrows had been known as such since at least 1296, and that these barrows were in fact the Ashen Hill Barrows. However, on the Tithe Map the field in which these Ashen Hill barrows and two of the Priddy Nine Barrows are situated was known as 'Nine Barrows Lot'. On the 1st edition Ordnance Survey map they are called 'Eight Barrows'. The Rev. John Skinner opened these barrows in the 19th century and found cremation burials, and thought that one of the barrows had been removed to provide material for a nearby wall. However, Grinsell believes he mistakenly assumed that these were the Priddy Nine Barrows.

The barrows are situated at a height of 295 metres OD and are arranged in an east-west line. They are all bowl barrows except for the fourth from the west which may be a bell barrow. They are all lower in height than in Skinner's day, and are between 1.5 metres and 2.7 metres in height and 18.3 metres to 21.3 metres in diameter. On the north (road) side of the barrows, deep hollows represent more recent mining activity.

Reading. Grinsell 1971, 71, 98-9, pl.1; Grinsell 1982.

Nearby sites. 108,113 Priddy; 111 Priddy Circles; 112 Priddy Nine Barrows.

4 ATHELNEY ABBEY (Saxon and Medieval monastery)

Location and parking   ST 346 292. Nine kilometres south-east of Bridgwater. A stone monument surrounded by railings marks the site, which is on farmland owned by Athelney Farm on the south side of the A361 Glastonbury-Taunton road, north-east of Lyng. The monument can be viewed on the crest of the hill from a large layby at ST 346 294. It can also be seen close-up: take the road from East Lyng to Athelney (Cuts Road), where there is room to park along the road by the bridge over the River Tone. Walk to the main unsignposted entrance of Athelney Farm and along the drive to the rear of the farmhouse; climb up the steps and at the top the monument can be viewed from the adjacent fence. This is not a

Athelney Abbey, the commemorative monument.

public right of way, but the farmer has given his kind consent for walkers on the North Curry Moor Trail to visit this monument.

Access for disabled visitors. The monument can be viewed from the layby along the A361.

Site description. The Athelney Monument was erected in 1801 by John Slade to mark the spot where King Alfred sought refuge from the Danes in 878 (and where he allegedly burnt the cakes) before defeating the Danes. Athelney is a small area of higher ground, which at that time was near the junction of the Rivers Parrett and Tone, surrounded by marshland, and could only be reached by boat. The course of the River Tone was later diverted in the Medieval period.

According to the contemporary writer Asser, an abbey was founded on the same spot by King Alfred about ten years later, although it is possible that Alfred enlarged an existing monastery. The early history of the abbey is obscure, but much more is known of its history from the time of the Conquest. It was a Benedictine monastery dedicated to St. Peter, St. Paul and St. Athelwine, but virtually nothing is known of the site's buildings and layout. In the early 12th century William of Malmesbury mentions a church, apparently built on four piers and with attached apsidal chapels. In 1321 the buildings were in a ruinous state, and in 1349 the abbey was badly affected by the Black Death, which caused the death of the abbot. Towards the end of the 15th century extensive repairs and possibly rebuilding are known to have been carried out.

The abbey was surrendered to the crown in 1539, and the building materials were valued at £80. In 1773 a vault was found in the area where the monument was later built, and a chapel is known to have existed nearby. The stone of the vault was removed and the cavity was filled in. During restoration of the 1801 monument by Somerset County Council in 1985, part of a tiled floor was found. There is also a commemorative plaque which is concealed by undergrowth between the layby and the A361 road.

Reading. Aston & Leech 1977, 87-91, maps 35, 36; Scott Holmes 1911, 99-103.

Nearby sites. 2 Aller; 18,19 Bridgwater; 22 Burrow Mump.

Axbridge, King John's Hunting Lodge.

5 AXBRIDGE, King John's Hunting Lodge (Museum and historic building)

Location ST 430 545. On the corner of Market Square and the High Street. The Square, Axbridge, BS26 2AP. Tel Axbridge (0934) 732012.

Parking. There is limited car parking in the square, or a pay car park in Moorland Street, two minutes walk from the museum.

Access for disabled visitors. There is only limited access downstairs with one small step at the entrance, but the exterior of the building can be viewed, with adjacent parking.

Facilities. There is a sales area. Refreshments and shops are available in the town, and there are toilets in Moorland Street.

Open. Daily 2pm-5pm, including Sundays and public holidays, from 1 April to 30 September. Parties by arrangement.

The Museum. The museum is housed in a National Trust timber-framed building, which was a late Medieval merchant's house built around 1400 and extensively restored in 1971. It is now a museum of local history and archaeology, run by Sedgemoor District Council in co-operation with Axbridge Archaeological & Local History Society. Originally the house had shops on the ground floor, dining quarters above and bedrooms on the top floor. Axbridge is likely to have been visited by King John, but this building which was not his hunting lodge was built long after his reign.

Reading. Pevsner 1958b, 81-2.

Nearby sites. 13 Black Down; 34 Cheddar; 35 Cheddar Gorge; 139 Tyning's Farm.

6 BALLANDS CASTLE, Penselwood
(Medieval castle)

Location and parking ST 753 310. 4.5 kilometres north-east of Wincanton. Take the north-eastwards turning off the current A303 road (by-pass in process of construction) to Penselwood at ST 751 299. Take the first left (north-west) turning, and after 600 metres there is very limited parking space near the old pump. Further up the road opposite a house called 'Kibitka' is a metal gate with a footpath signposted to Penselwood Forest. Go down the short stretch of trackway; from here the footpath goes straight across the field. Cross the next stile, and the castle earthworks are visible from the footpath.

Access for disabled visitors. None.

Site description. The site of Ballands Castle consists of the substantial earthworks of a motte and bailey castle, which was constructed on the north end of a slight ridge. A rectangular enclosure to the south was probably the bailey.

Reading. Bothamley 1911, 515-16; Burrow 1924, 122, 123 (figure)

Nearby sites. 20 Bruton; 74 Horsington; 82 Kenwalch's Castle; 126 Stavordale Priory.

7 BATTLEGORE, Williton
(Round barrows and a stone setting)

Location ST 074 416. Just NNW of Williton in North Street (B3191, St. Decumans to Williton road) in fields opposite the Danesfield Church of England School. One round barrow with a ditch is situated just to the south of the stream and can be viewed from the gateway to the field adjacent to the layby. Near the next field right by the hedge are two large and two smaller stones. In the next field immediately opposite the school entrance is a large round barrow, situated quite close to the hedge alongside the road. Further south in the same field is another round barrow, situated at the rear of the houses and beneath overhead power lines. This barrow is visible from the footpath alongside the road.

Parking. In a layby on the south side of the road opposite the school.

Access for disabled visitors. Part of the site can be viewed from the field gateway at the layby.

Site description. There are three round barrows and a stone setting. The round barrows are probably all Bronze Age in date, while the stone setting may belong to a Neolithic long barrow, since destroyed.

There are two large Old Red Sandstone stones (approx 1.8 metres in length) and two smaller ones. The site was excavated in 1931 when socket holes were found at the foot of two stones, suggesting that they were once upright, and that a third stone may have been a covering slab. Several smaller stones were also found. They may have formed an entrance to a Neolithic long barrow, which had been destroyed before the 1931 excavations. There was evidence for Bronze Age burials covered by the round barrows, with a female cremation in a pottery urn being discovered in 1931, but no evidence for burials within the possible long barrow was found.

The megalithic stones are said to have been thrown into their present position as the result of a contest between the Devil and a giant (probably the Giant of Grabbist Hill at Dunster). One of the large stones was apparently upright in the mid 19th century, but was pushed against the hedge by some young men trying to test the truth of the legend that it was immovable. The field is now known as Battlegore, but previously the site has been known as Bytelgore, Gradborough and Grabburrows ('grave barrows').

Reading. Gray, 1932 (including a plan of part of the site); Grinsell 1969, 3, 6, 13, 26, 41; Grinsell 1976a, 98.

Nearby sites. 38 Cleeve Abbey; 44 Daw's Castle; 137 Trendle Ring; 142 Watchet.

8 BAT'S CASTLE (Iron Age hillfort)

Location SS 987 421. 1.25 kilometres SSW of Dunster. This hillfort is 0.5 kilometres south-east of Black Ball Camp and is easily visited on the same trip. It is situated on the southern summit of Gallox Hill, and can be reached on foot from Dunster. From Black Ball Camp, return along the path downhill to where there is a junction with the footpath leading to Dunster. Continue along the path uphill for 350 metres, when it passes across the southern part of the hillfort. Allow two hours to visit Bat's Castle, Black Ball Camp and the Gallox Hill linear earthwork.

Parking. There is a pay car park at Mill Gardens near the Gallox Bridge in Dunster.

Access for disabled visitors. None.

Facilities. There are toilets, refreshments, shops and banks in Dunster.

Site description. This hillfort is situated at 205 metres OD on the highest point of Gallox Hill. In the past it has also been known as Caesar's Camp, and there are fine views from the site. The hillfort was probably associated with Black Ball Camp. It consists of two ramparts of stone and two ditches, the one between the two ramparts still being clearly visible. The ramparts survive to a height of about 2.5 metres. The substantial defences enclose a roughly circular area of one hectare, and there are entrances on the west and east sides. At the west entrance the inner bank is turned inwards, but at the east entrance the outer bank is turned outwards to form a passage 23 metres long, an unusual feature and one which may not be original. The ramparts have been damaged in places, and much of the hillfort is covered in scrub and other vegetation.

Reading. Burrow 1924, 84, 85 (figure); Burrow 1981, 242-3; Grinsell 1970, plate on p.72.

Nearby sites. 12 Black Ball Camp; 52, 53 Dunster; 64 Gallox Hill.

9 BEACON BATCH, Black Down
(Bronze Age round barrows)

Location and parking ST 484 572. Four kilometres north-east of Cheddar. The barrows are sited on the highest part of the Black Down ridge (325 metres OD). There is a large layby at the eastern end of Burrington Combe on a bend on the north side of the B3134 road at ST 489 581. Walk up the road (south-eastwards) for 125 metres and along the unmarked footpath leading southwards along a rough trackway by the side of Ellick House. After 300 metres the trackway emerges into open moorland at a point where three public rights of way converge. Take the footpath that goes straight up the hillside (south-westwards). Towards the summit the barrows become visible.

Access for disabled visitors. None.

Site description. Beacon Batch barrow cemetery is a group of ten round barrows clustered on the crest of the hill, although only seven barrows are now clearly visible. A barely visible barrow on the west of the group has been recorded as a Neolithic long barrow, but this is a dubious identification. The most prominent round barrow is surmounted by a concrete pillar for a trigonometrical point. The barrows have hollows in them, showing that they have been dug into, but unfortunately without record. One of the barrows is known to have been opened by Rev. J. Skinner in 1820. The name 'Batch' refers to the piece of ground on which the barrows are situated.

Across Black Down are a series of small mounds covered in vegetation in long double rows running east-west and north-south. They resemble complex alignments of prehistoric stone rows that appear to be associated with the barrows. In fact, they are decoy mounds of peat which are now decaying but were originally about 1.5 metres high. They were constructed during the 1939-1945 war from Charterhouse to Shipham as a decoy for enemy aircraft so that the rows resembled railway lines or a town. The mounds each had dim lamps which could be switched on to represent 'black-out' lighting. Several masses of inflammable material were also present to be lit to represent fires in a town. As far as is known these decoy mounds had little effect.

Reading. Aston & Murless (eds) 1978, 140-1; Grinsell 1971, 57, 71, 81 (figure), 93; Tratman 1966.

Nearby sites. 13 Black Down; 31, 33 Charterhouse-on-Mendip; 139 Tyning's Farm.

10 BEACON HILL, near Shepton Mallet
(Bronze Age round barrows)

Location ST 633 461 to 641 458. Three kilometres north-east of Shepton Mallet. The site is on the south side of the Old Frome Road, 500 metres south-east of the junction of this road with the A37 road. Part of the site lies within the Forestry Commission's Beacon Hill Wood, Mendip Forest, but the barrows are not visible from the

Bronze Age cremation urn in a stone cist from the Beacon Hill barrows, near Shepton Mallet

bridleway through the forest. From the road, four barrows can be seen in the field to the west of the forest – three are close to the road and can be seen from the gate at the west end of the field (at ST 633 463). The fourth barrow is barely visible as a low mound right by the forest boundary.

Parking. There is limited roadside parking, and also room to park at the entrance to the forest if it is not in use and if access is not blocked.

Access for disabled visitors. The barrows can be seen from the roadside.

Site description. The Beacon Hill barrow cemetery near Shepton Mallet is a linear cemetery of Bronze Age barrows situated on the ridge line. There may once have been at least 17 barrows – eight in the field (four adjoining), and nine in the forest. None are very high, and ones in the forest have been affected by tree planting and are inaccessible. Only four barrows in the field are now visible from the road.

The barrows were mainly dug into by the Rev. John Skinner in the early 19th century, with some subsequent activity in the 1950's when the forest was being planted. Because of his excavation techniques (appalling by today's standards), the Rev. Skinner obtained very little information. The barrows mainly contained cremations, some in stone cists and pottery cremation urns. At least one of the barrows was used in recent centuries as a beacon.

Reading. Grinsell 1971, 53, 57, 58, 62, 71, 74, 80 (plan of barrows), 88, 104.

Nearby sites. 14 Blacker's Hill; 88 Maesbury Castle; 149, 150 Whitnell Corner.

Bicknoller, see **Trendle Ring**.

11 BISHOPS LYDEARD (Medieval crosses)

Location   ST 167 297. In the west end of the churchyard of the parish church of St. Mary the Virgin at Bishop's Lydeard.

Parking. Take the lane by the police station leading off Church Street, and there is a small car park between the Bell Inn and the butchers shop, next to the churchyard. Alternatively, there is some roadside parking in Church Street by the church.

Access for disabled visitors. Access is possible from the car park, but there is wider access from the main Church Street entrance.

Facilities. Toilets are situated by the health centre at the west end of this large village. There are also shops and banks.

Site description. There are two crosses in the churchyard. One is a 14th century cross with

Bishops Lydeard, churchyard cross.

carved figures around the octagonal socket and another on the east face of the shaft. This cross is constructed on three steps, and the figures around the socket include the Twelve Apostles, while the one on the shaft was apparently of St. John the Baptist. The cross has deteriorated since Pooley described it over a century ago.

Close-by are the remains of an old market cross, which once stood in the village but was moved to the churchyard over a century ago. It consists of three octagonal steps, a low socket, and a fragment of the shaft.

Note also the fine early 16th century carved bench ends in the church itself, especially the ship and the windmill.

Reading. Pooley 1877, 90-3.

Nearby sites. 42 Crowcombe; 102 Norton Fitzwarren; 105 Plainsfield Camp; 134 Taunton.

12 BLACK BALL CAMP (Iron Age hillfort)

Location SS 984 426. One kilometre south-west of Dunster. The hillfort is situated on the northern summit of Gallox Hill, and can be reached on foot from Dunster. Cross over the Gallox Bridge, and go past the thatched cottages up to the wooden gates (a large one and a smaller pedestrian one). Go through the gates, and just in front is a signpost. Turn right (marked to Withycombe on the wrong face of the signpost) along the red waymarked route which follows a valley uphill through the woods. Keep straight ahead, and the path then emerges into open moorland with bracken. It then joins a wider, stoney path, at which point turn right (north). Continue uphill for 175 metres, and the hillfort is on the left (west) adjacent to the path.

Parking. There is a pay car park at Mill Gardens near the Gallox Bridge in Dunster.

Access for disabled visitors. None.

Facilities. There are toilets, refreshments, shops and banks in Dunster.

Site description. This hillfort is situated on sandstone moorland at 160 metres OD and is also known as Gallox Hill or British Camp. The impressive rampart and ditch can still be seen, now covered in bracken, heather and scrub, and enclosing an area of 0.3 hectares. The rampart is about three metres high and the ditch is two metres

deep. A single entrance was on the south-west at the steepest approach to the hillfort. From the top of the rampart, the whole circuit can be seen, as well as Bat's Castle on the summit to the south-east with which Black Ball Camp is likely to have been associated. At the beginning of this century, the foundations of a stone tower were visible. There are fine views from the hillfort.

Reading. Burrow 1924, 106, 107 (figure); Burrow 1981, 256.

Nearby sites. 8 Bat's Castle; 52, 53 Dunster; 64 Gallox Hill.

Black Down, see also **Beacon Batch.**

13 BLACK DOWN
(Bronze Age round barrows)

Location and parking ST 473 571. 3.5 kilometres north-east of Cheddar. A group of three round barrows is situated one kilometre WSW of the Beacon Batch barrows, from which there is a well-worn path. Just before the junction with the north-south path from Tyning's Farm, two barrows are visible on the north side of the path, but the barrow on the south side is not visible.

An alternative route is to walk from Tyning's Farm (near where there is limited roadside parking) at ST 470 565. Take the worn path which goes up the steep hillside for 350 metres to a stile and gate. Cross the stile, and there is an old air raid shelter on the left (west). Continue up the hill for nearly one kilometre, and the barrows are along the path on the right.

Access for disabled visitors. None.

Site description. These three Bronze Age round barrows are situated at the western end of the Black Down ridge at 309 metres OD. The barrow to the south of the path was considered by Grinsell to be doubtful, and is no longer visible.

Reading. Grinsell 1971, 93.

Nearby sites. 9 Beacon Batch; 35 Cheddar Gorge; 118 Rowberrow; 139 Tyning's Farm.

14 BLACKER'S HILL, Chilcompton
(Iron Age hillfort)

Location ST 636 501. 4.5 kilometres south-west of Radstock. At the southern end of Downside, 300 metres south of the school, take a sharp right turn into Coalpit Lane. 300 metres further along there is room to park opposite the un-signposted lane to Blacker's Hill Farm. At the entrance to the lane is a large white gate and two white posts, with metal field gates on either side. Walk along the lane, and as it curves to the right, the substantial hillfort ramparts are in front, with another stretch visible from the field gate on the left where the ramparts have been cut through.

The footpath continues up the lane alongside the ramparts, and over the cattle grid. After a distance of 100 metres, there is a gap in the ramparts on the left (south) with a metal field gate. Go through the gate into the field. The ramparts are in places quite overgrown, but they are visible from the footpath around part of this field. Cross the field southwards to the metal field gate opposite, and go into the next field. Turn left (east) and follow the field boundary to the next metal gate in the north-east corner of the field. Go through this gate, and the footpath passes through a gap in the ramparts which is probably the original entrance. On the left the ramparts are overgrown, but on the right (south) two ramparts and a ditch are clearly visible (a second, outer ditch being barely visible). Follow the line of the ramparts southwards to the corner of this field. At this point the ramparts stop, and a very steep drop can be seen where the hillfort has been built on a promontory.

Access for disabled visitors. It may be possible in dry weather to negotiate the footpath along the lane as far as the ramparts by the cattle grid, but parking is only possible on the nearby road.

Site description. Blacker's Hill is a roughly rectangular Iron Age hillfort at a height of 215 metres OD. The hillfort is a promontory fort, and on the west and south sides it is not defended by ramparts but by the very steep natural drop to the river valley below. It covers six hectares, and was originally defended by two ramparts and two ditches, with the inner rampart being lower in height than the outer one. In places the ramparts survive to a considerable height, but on the north-east side, the inner rampart and ditch have been destroyed. The defences are now used as field boundaries, parts of which are overgrown and wooded. There are three gaps through the

defences, but only the one on the east seems to be the original entrance.

Reading. Burrow 1924, 70, 71 (figure showing the defences not overgrown); Burrow 1981, 212, pl.2

Nearby sites. 10 Beacon Hill; 88 Maesbury Castle; 149, 150 Whitnell Corner.

Blackmoor Nature Reserve, see Charterhouse-on-Mendip.

15 BLUE GATE, Exmoor (Bronze Age barrow)

Location SS 755 375. Two kilometres south-west of Simonsbath. Take the road south-westwards from Simonsbath to Kinsford Gate Cross. After nearly 1.5 kilometres, go past the turning on the left at Blue Gate signposted 'Wintershead & Horsen'. The barrow is in the adjacent field, on the left (south) side of the road, 300 metres south-west of the Blue Gate turning. It is in the north-west corner of the field, by the gate and the field boundary.

Parking. There is limited roadside parking.

Access for disabled visitors. The mound is visible from the field gate by the road.

Site description. This low isolated Bronze Age round barrow is now about one metre in height and ten metres in diameter.

Reading. Grinsell 1969, 33.

Nearby sites. 41 Cow Castle; 71 Green Barrow and Brightworthy Barrows; 138 Two Barrows; 141 Wambarrows.

16 BREAN DOWN (Iron Age hillfort, prehistoric barrows and field systems)

Location ST 287 589. Three kilometres south-west of Weston-super-Mare. Situated at the end of the coast road from Berrow and Brean. Brean Down is reached by two steep footpaths – one consisting of steps, and a less steep path to the east.

Parking. A privately-owned pay car park is situated at the end of the coast road (at ST 296 587).

Access for disabled visitors. Brean Down can be viewed from the car park, but none of the individual archaeological sites can be reached.

Brean Down, a view of the promontory.

Plan of the main archaeological sites on Brean Down.

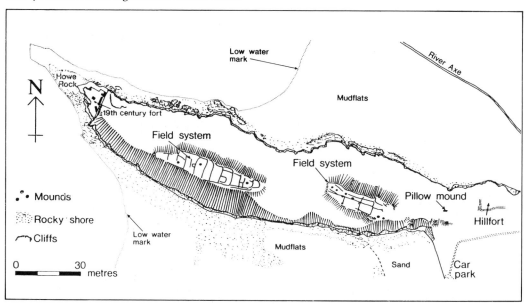

Facilities. There is a privately-owned cafe (with toilets) and shops by the car park.

Site description. Brean Down is a steep-sided limestone promontory (an extension of the Mendips) which extends 1.6 kilometres into the Bristol Channel, and is owned by the National Trust. Many archaeological features survive, but some are no longer visible, and others have been excavated, both on the ridge and below the cliffs. There is visible disturbance caused by 19th and 20th century military activity.

Brean Down seems to have been occupied from at least the Bronze Age, when its woodland was probably cleared for the first time for agriculture. It may have been an island, at least at high tides. There are several circular mounds on the promontory, some being Bronze Age round barrows, while others seem more likely to be field clearance cairns associated with the field systems (representing the clearance of stones from the fields during ploughing). Not all the mounds are distinct.

The east footpath leads to a small Iron Age promontory hillfort with a rampart running east-west alongside the footpath on the ridge, and then turning north-south with an accompanying ditch on the west. The ramparts originally consisted of rubble banks faced at the front and rear with massive stone walls, but the masonry structure is no longer visible. To the west is a Post-Medieval pillow mound.

Further west, on the south side of the footpath, there are round barrows which are visible as grass-covered mounds. They are probably Bronze Age in date, and around them the raised banks form part of a field system. In this area a Roman temple was excavated, but its site is not visible.

Further along the footpath, beyond a wire fence with a wooden stile is another field system, visible as a series of mainly north-south linear ridges up to one metre in height, which are possibly of Iron Age or Roman date. Beyond this are several mounds, some of which may be prehistoric barrows or field clearance mounds. At the tip of the promontory is a 19th century military fort.

Reading. Bell 1990; Burrow 1981, 249-51; Grinsell 1971, 91-2.

Nearby sites. 5 Axbridge; 17 Brent Knoll; 46 Downend; 118 Rowberrow.

17 BRENT KNOLL (Iron Age hillfort)

Location and parking ST 341 509. Eight kilometres south of Weston-super-Mare. Steep public footpaths converge on Brent Knoll from all directions. The best route is to take the road from

Brent Knoll hillfort, aerial view (photo by M. Aston).

East Brent to Brent Knoll village. A field opposite the entrance to Manor Farm (at ST 335 513) by a private road to Windy Ridge is set aside for a car park. (Alternatively at Brent Knoll village, turn off the B3140 road (Brent Street) up Church Lane (signposted 'to the knoll'), turn left and Manor Farm is on the right and the car park is on the left). Follow the signposted footpath, past Manor Farm and through the farmyard. Proceed to the gate and stile, across the next field as far as the top right-hand corner where there is a National Trust sign and a stile. A series of steps leads to the top of the ramparts.

Access for disabled visitors. None, although the hillfort can be viewed from a distance.

Site description. Brent Knoll is situated on a prominent Lias sandstone island rising to a height of 139 metres OD above the surrounding Levels. It is now in the care of the National Trust. It is an Iron Age hillfort, which has also produced evidence for Roman occupation extending to the 4th century. It encloses an area of 1.6 hectares, with an inner bank (discontinuous where it has been partly quarried away) and a ditch. There is a second major bank part-way down the hillside. The original entrance was on the east side, and on the west and south sides the hill has been artificially shaped by terracing, some of which is possibly Medieval in origin. The interior has been damaged by extensive quarrying for the Lias limestone which caps the hill. Quarrying was mentioned by the Rev. J. Skinner when he undertook excavations on the site in 1812. Quarrying has lowered the level of the interior of the hillfort by at least two metres, and on the north side the outer defences have been used for military trenches in recent times. From the top of the hill there are spectacular views across the Somerset Levels.

Reading. Burrow 1981, 72-3, 236-8, 295-300, pls. 5, 11, plan A.

Nearby sites. 5 Axbridge; 16 Brean Down; 46 Downend; 143 Wedmore.

18 BRIDGWATER (Medieval castle)

Location ST 299 372. The only visible parts of the castle are along West Quay by the River Parrett. The Water Gate is set back from the road down a passage along the north side of The

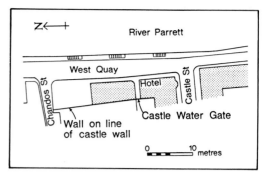

Location of the visible remains of Bridgwater Castle.

Watergate Hotel, midway between Castle Street and Chandos Street. Further along towards Chandos Street is a stretch of the masonry curtain wall.

Parking. There are several pay car parks in the town, and limited parking in adjacent streets. West Quay has a no parking restriction.

Access for disabled visitors. The Water Gate and the nearby wall are accessible from the pavement alongside West Quay, although parking outside these sites could block access to other traffic.

Site description. The castle was built around 1200 by William de Briwerre, of whom was written, in *A Pilgrim's Poem*:

He built the Castle in this town,
The bridge he built besides;
His charity bears high renown,
'Tis like the Parret's tides.

The castle appears to have been a rectangular enclosure in the area of Chandos Street and Castle Street, with King Square being on the site of the bailey. Leland (around 1540-42) said 'The Castelle sumtyme a right fair and strong Peace of Worke, but now al goyng to mere Ruine'. It was fortified by the Royalists in 1645 during the Civil War, but fell to the Parliamentarians in July 1645 and was largely demolished. Only the Water Gate and a stretch of curtain wall fronting the quay survive as visible remains. The single arched gateway of the Water Gate is built of stone with some later brickwork and is probably of 13th century date. It is poorly presented as a monument. Further along towards Chandos Street is a tall stretch of wall, once part of the castle wall.

Reading. Aston & Leech 1977, 15, pl. 1, map 5.

Nearby sites. 19 Bridgwater; 22 Burrow Mump; 46 Downend; 125 Spaxton.

19 BRIDGWATER, Admiral Blake Museum

Location ST 301 368. Museum House, Blake Street, Bridgwater. Tel. Bridgwater (0278) 456127.

Parking. There are several nearby pay car parks in the town, the closest being at the junction of George Street and Dampiet Street.

Access for disabled visitors. There is access to the archaeology displays on the ground floor with parking outside the museum.

Facilities. There is a sales area in the museum. Refreshments, banks and toilets are available in the town.

Open. All year, including the lunch hour. Monday to Saturday 11am-5pm (8pm on Wednesday), Sunday 2-5pm.

The Museum. This museum is administered by Sedgemoor District Council and is manned by volunteers. It occupies the house which was the birthplace of Admiral Robert Blake (1598-1657), Cromwell's chief admiral. The building itself dates from around 1500, and is in Blake Street, previously named Mill Lane. There are displays on all archaeological periods, with finds from Bridgwater and the locality, with a new archaeology gallery.

Reading. *Official guide to the Admiral Blake Museum 1986* (available from the museum).

Nearby sites. 18 Bridgwater; 22 Burrow Mump; 46 Downend; 125 Spaxton.

Brightworthy Barrows, see **Green Barrow and Brightworthy Barrows**.

20 BRUTON (Medieval priory wall)

Location ST 684 347. A high stone wall is visible along the south side of the street known as the Plox (running westwards from the church).

Parking. Limited roadside parking is available in the road opposite St. Mary's parish church.

Access for disabled visitors. The priory wall runs along the road and is accessible at all times.

Site description. The Augustinian priory at Bruton was founded around 1130, although there is evidence for an earlier monastery. The Medieval town was on the opposite side of the river and had a planned regular layout of streets, but the parish church was near the priory buildings. There may possibly have been a separate priory church. The

13th century seal of Bruton Priory.

priory was surrendered to the crown on 1st April 1539, and after the dissolution the priory buildings were sold to the Berkeley family. Some of the buildings to the south of the parish church were converted to a large mansion, which was demolished in the late 18th century. Excavations have taken place, but little of the priory is now visible, and the area is now mainly playing fields. The heavily buttressed high stone wall along the Plox is part of the original precinct wall. The nearby dovecote is often quoted as belonging to the priory, but it appears to be of later date.

Reading. Aston & Leech 1977, 20, 21, map 7; Colt Hoare 1824, 40-102; Scott Holmes 1911, 134-8.

Nearby sites. 26 Castle Cary; 82 Kenwalch's Castle; 124 Spargrove; 126 Stavordale Priory.

21 BRYMPTON HOUSE, Brympton D'Evercy (Roman mosaic)

Location and parking ST 520 154. 2.5 kilometres west of Yeovil. The house is reached from the Yeovil to Odcombe road – follow the signs to Brympton House from the A30 or A303 roads. There is a large free car park. Between the house and Church is the Priest House in which the mosaic is displayed upstairs, on the first floor. Brympton Estate Office, Yeovil, Somerset, BA22 8TD. Tel. West Coker (093586) 2528.

Access for disabled visitors. No access is possible to the mosaic on the first floor.

Facilities. There is a shop, small restaurant and toilets.

Admission charge. There is an admission charge to the historic house, with discounts for senior citizens and National Trust members Mondays-Wednesdays.

Open. Easter Friday, Saturday, Sunday and Monday, and then 1 May to 30 September every afternoon (except Thursdays and Fridays) 2pm-6pm.

The Museum. The Priest House is a 13th century building which functions as the sales area and has a cider making display. Upstairs is a tessellated Roman pavement of blue lias limestone and red tile which was until recently in the municipal offices. It was excavated in 1923 by Ralegh Radford from a building near Westland Road in Yeovil. Several other similar floors were found in the same building, which is usually referred to as the Westland Roman villa, but may have been part of a small rural settlement spread over a fairly extensive area rather than a typical villa.

Reading. Leech & Leach 1982, 73, fig. 8.16 (for the Westland site); Radford 1929 (plate c.2 shows the mosaic in situ).

Nearby sites. 95, 96, 97 Montacute; 160 Yeovil.

22 BURROW MUMP, Burrowbridge
(Church ruins on top of hill)

Location and parking ST 358 305. Seven kilometres south-east of Bridgwater. On the south side of the A361 road at Burrowbridge is a car park at the east side of the prominent hill at ST 360 305. A footpath leads from the car park across the stile to the top of the hill. There is also a footpath from the village of Burrowbridge on the west side of the hill.

Access for disabled visitors. The monument is visible from the car park.

Site description. The site is in the care of the National Trust, and was presented by Major A. G. Barrett in 1946 as a war memorial through the Somerset War Memorial Fund. Burrow Mump,

Illustration of Burrow Mump drawn in 1762.

also known as St. Michael's Borough or Tutteyate, is a natural hill of Triassic sandstone capped by Keuper Marl. Part of it appears to be terraced, but this is due largely to its geological formation, with some artificial scarping at the top of the hill where the church is situated. It is almost 24 metres in height, yet only 31 metres above sea level. Until the drainage of this part of the Somerset Levels from the Medieval period, Burrow Mump was frequently an island rising above the floods.

The site is in a strong strategic position, at the confluence of the River Tone and the former course of the River Cary with the River Parrett. It was traditionally called 'King Alfred's Fort' but there is no evidence to substantiate this claim. Excavations showed evidence for a 12th century masonry building on top of the hill, which was interpreted as a possible castle. One of the earliest references to Burrow Mump is that written by William of Worcestre in about 1480, when he referred to it as 'Myghell-borough'. A Medieval church dedicated to St. Michael existed on the site from at least the mid 15th century and is depicted in a ruinous condition in two mid 18th century engravings. By 1645 the church was in a ruinous condition, in which year 120 Royalist troops sought refuge in the ruined church from where they soon surrendered. A new chapel began to be built at the end of the 18th century but work was not finished. The chapel was never consecrated, and instead another church was built at the foot of Burrow Mump and consecrated in 1836. The ruins of the 18th century church are visible today, and there are extensive views from the top of the hill.

Reading. *Burrow Mump, Somerset* (a leaflet produced by the National Trust); Gray 1940.

Nearby sites. 2 Aller; 4 Athelney Abbey; 18, 19 Bridgwater.

23 BURY CASTLE, Selworthy
(Iron Age hillfort)

Location and parking SS 917 471.
2.75 kilometres ENE of Porlock. From the A39 road take the turning north-eastwards to Selworthy. At Selworthy there is a National Trust car park at the end of the road at SS 920 467 (closes at 7.30pm), or an overflow car park opposite the church. Walk back to the gate leading into Selworthy Green (the National Trust village), but do not take the footpath on the right signposted to Bury Castle. Go through the gate and past the National Trust shop. Cross the stream into Selworthy Woods using the stone slab bridge with a wooden handrail, signposted 'Bossington 2, Hurlestone 3'. Walk along the path for 30 metres, turn left, and go over a stile. After another 30 metres there is a signpost to Bury Castle, but its direction is confusing. Do not continue up the main grassy track, but bear right up some small, rough stone steps and turn left along the indistinct higher path. Go up this narrow path which becomes more distinct, and turn right, signposted to Bury Castle, continuing uphill. The path then bears sharply right and goes up to a drystone wall with a stile. Go over the stile and up the steep slope signposted to Bury Castle. The path emerges into open ground with scrub and bracken. Turn right and the hillfort is in front. West of the main ramparts, the path crosses another large rampart and ditch, and further west it crosses a smaller rampart and ditch.

Access for disabled visitors. None.

Facilities. There are refreshments at Selworthy Green. Toilets are situated nearly opposite the Tithe Barn along the road on the south side of the village, and are signposted from Selworthy Green.

Site description. The Iron Age hillfort of Bury Castle is on the eastern end of a promontory, and the ramparts enclose 0.2 hectares. The whole circuit of the ramparts can be walked, although they are rather overgrown with bracken in places. The main enclosure has a single rampart and ditch, with steep drops on the north, south and east sides. The defences are still very prominent in places. Thirty metres to the west a substantial rampart runs across the ridge, strengthening the defences on this side. On its west side is a deep ditch. The rampart is revetted with drystone walling, visible in places to the north of the footpath. 150 metres further west is a smaller bank and ditch, largely overgrown with bracken and gorse, but it is thought that this may be a later field boundary and not part of the hillfort defences.

Reading. Burrow 1924, 72, 73 (figure); Burrow 1981, 259-60; Grinsell 1970, 79, 84-5.

Nearby sites. 73 Horner; 120 Selworthy; 121 Selworthy Beacon; 148 West Luccombe.

Cadbury Camelot, see **South Cadbury Castle.**

24 CARATACUS STONE, Winsford Hill
(Dark Age memorial stone)

Location SS 889 335. Two kilometres south-west of Winsford on Exmoor. From Winsford, the stone is on the left-hand side of the road (Halse Lane) just before the junction with the B3223 road at Spire Cross. The stone is in a shelter 100 metres off the road. The land is owned by the National Trust.

Parking. Parking is possible close to the road.

Access for disabled visitors. Difficult, as the moor path to the stone is soft and very uneven.

Site description. The Latin inscription on the stone, CARAACI ИEPVS, reads downwards, and can be transcribed as CARATACI NEPUS: descendant of Caratacus (Caradog). It dates to the Dark Ages around AD 500. The letters RG also occur faintly beneath the inscription, carved at an unknown later date. Many photographs show the inscription with white lettering, the lettering having been touched up. It is likely that part of the inscription is missing, including the name of the person being commemorated. The stone itself is of local sandstone, and is 1.5 metres high. Many traditions surround the stone, including that of buried treasure, and many strange events are alleged to have occurred in the vicinity, such as waggons inexplicably smashing against the stone.

The stone can be traced as far back as 1219 in documents, because it was used as a boundary landmark. It may have been moved from its original position for this purpose. In the Medieval perambulations of Exmoor in 1219 and 1279, the stone was known as 'Langeston' (Longstone). It was first recognised in 1890, during which year a labourer vandalised the stone with a pick, damaging the first C and knocking off the reversed N. The Rev. J. Coleman, Curate of Dulverton, apparently found the piece with the 'N' and buried it nearby for safety. In 1906 Sir Thomas Acland, then owner of Winsford Hill, had a shelter built over the site. The missing N was retrieved by Jim Weetch, a local keeper, when constructing the shelter, and the stone was subsequently restored. In 1918 Sir Thomas Acland leased the site to the National Trust for 500 years. In 1936 the stone

Caratacus Stone before restoration.

was once again vandalised, this time by prising the 356 kilogram object out of the ground. This was a formidable undertaking, and was presumably done in the hope of finding the legendary hidden treasure. Before re-erecting the stone, the area was excavated, but nothing was found, and the stone was cemented in place.

Reading. Bryant 1984; Fowler 1988, 11; Grinsell 1970, 104, 125 (photograph); Vowles 1939.

Nearby sites. 70 Great Rowbarrow and Little Rowbarrow; 71 Green Barrow and Brightworthy Barrows; 132 Tarr Steps; 156 Withypool.

25 CART GATE, near Martock
(Ridge-and-furrow)

Location and parking ST 470 184. Ridge-and-furrow is visible on the north side of the A303 road between Martock and Stoke-sub-Hamdon. It is situated in two small fields immediately to the north and west of Cart Gate farmhouse, on the west side of the road from Martock to Stoke-sub-Hamdon. The best viewpoint is from the elevated part of the latter road, just to the north of the slip road to the A303 road before it crosses over the A303. It is possible to stop along the roadside.

Access for disabled visitors. The ridge-and-furrow can be seen from the road.

Site description. The ridge-and-furrow consists of parallel linear ridges, and represents the remains of a field system of probable Medieval date.

Reading. Whitfield 1981 (field systems in south-east Somerset).

Nearby sites. 39 Coat; 72 Ham Hill; 97 Montacute; 128 Stoke-sub-Hamdon.

26 CASTLE CARY (Medieval castle)

Location ST 641 321. Walk along the small passageway called Paddock Drain (opposite Market Place) and follow the tarmac footpath (signposted to Lodge Hill), up some steps and over the stile. At this point there are two divergent footpaths across the fields. Take the left-hand (south-east) footpath which follows the field boundary and crosses a substantial embankment and ditch, possibly part of the castle bailey. Return along the same path to the stile, and follow the other unmarked footpath southwards (which crosses the field diagonally). On the right-hand (west) side is a moat surrounding a large mound.

Parking. There is a car park off Park Street, near the garage and fire station.

Access for disabled visitors. The bailey earthworks are visible from the car park, and the motte from Park Place (a cul-de-sac off Park Street), but they are difficult to identify as they are dominated by the ridge behind. There are toilets in the car park.

Facilities. There are refreshments, shops and banks in the town, and toilets in the car park.

Site description. The castle today consists of large embankments, possibly part of a bailey surrounding a motte (mound). In 1890 the foundations of a substantial stone-built keep were excavated on top of this mound. This was a tower 24 metres square, with a cross wall, and was constructed of rubble faced with ashlar masonry. Two stone markers (originally four) mark the position of the keep (see Hershon 1990, pl.v). It was originally a Norman castle, probably of some importance and built in the late 11th or early 12th century. It was besieged twice in King Stephen's reign, in 1138 and 1148, and was probably destroyed after about 1153. Many of the buildings in Castle Cary are apparently constructed of stone from the castle, including two decorative corbels on the Market Hall which are reputed to come from the castle.

Reading. Aston & Leech 1977, 27-30, maps 10, 11; Hershon 1990.

Nearby sites. 20 Bruton; 36 Clanville; 56 East Lydford; 124 Spargrove.

Site of the castle at Castle Cary as surveyed in 1890.

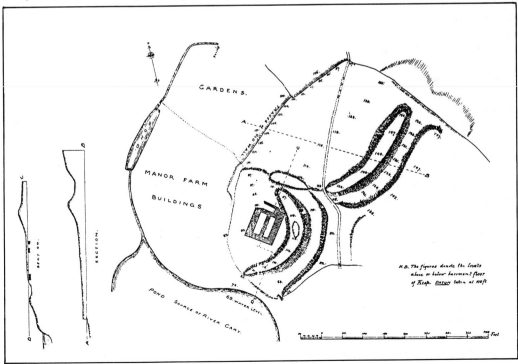

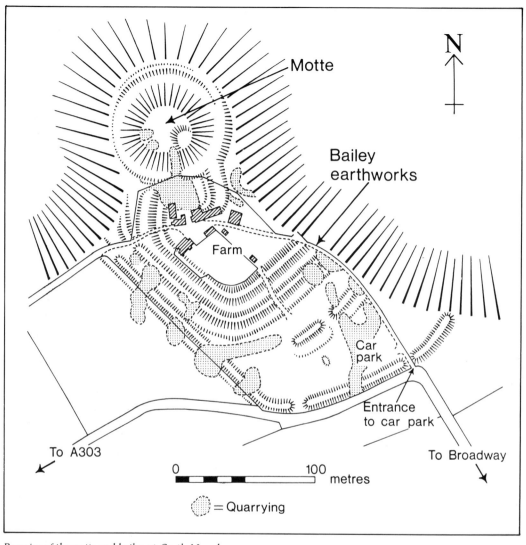

N

Motte

Bailey
earthworks

Farm

Car
park

Entrance
to car park

To A303

To Broadway

0   100
                          metres

⬭ = Quarrying

Remains of the motte and bailey at Castle Neroche.

27 CASTLE NEROCHE (Medieval castle)

Location and parking ST 271 158.
8.5 kilometres west of Ilminster. The castle is
situated on the north-eastern tip of the Blackdown
Hills. It can be reached from the narrow road from
Broadway. Turn right at the junction and after a
few yards turn right into the Forestry Commission
car park. Alternatively approach from the A303
road, and after 2.5 kilometres turn right (opposite a
sign pointing left to Bracken Lodge Farm), and
then after 350 metres yards turn left into the car
park.

Access for disabled visitors. Some of the site
can be seen from the car park which is situated
within the earthworks of the castle.

Facilities. A nature trail and picnic area are open
at all times.

Site description. A castle was built in the 11th
century, probably by Robert, Count of Mortain,
King William's half-brother and holder of Montacute. A series of ditches and ramparts was constructed across a spur of the Blackdown Hills, and
these are still visible. The castle may have been
built on the site of an earlier Iron Age hillfort,

although evidence for this is inconclusive – the outermost earthwork may be of Iron Age date, or of Saxon date. In the 12th century a 6-7.5 metre high motte was constructed, converting the site to a motte-and-bailey castle. The motte was 36 metres in diameter at its summit. A masonry shell-keep was also constructed in one corner of the motte, but none of its masonry walls are visible. Excavations on the site were undertaken in 1903 and 1961-64, and evidence showed that the castle went out of use in the 12th century.

The largest rampart is the inner bank and ditch with an entrance now leading to Castle Neroche Farm which occupies part of the area within the earthworks. Some of the site has been destroyed by 19th century quarrying.

Reading. Burrow 1924, 126-8 (including figures); Davison 1972; Gray 1904.

Nearby sites. 29 Chard Museum; 117 Robin Hood's Butts; 133, 136 Taunton.

Castle Wood, see **Kenwalch's Castle**

28 CHAPEL CROSS, St. Andrew's Chapel
(Medieval chapel ruins)

Location SS 905 448. 2.5 kilometres south-east of Porlock. The chapel ruins are situated on the north-east side of the road from Horner to Luccombe. From Luccombe, go through the Chapel Cross crossroads, and the ruins are on a small green on the right of the road, just past the first field and by the gate to that field. The ruins are surrounded by wooden posts about 0.5 metres high.

Parking. There is roadside parking next to the ruins.

Access for disabled visitors. Parking is possible adjacent to the monument.

Site description. Only the wall foundations of the chapel are visible, standing up to 0.4 metres in height. The chapel was rectangular in shape, measuring about 8 metres x 4.5 metres, with the walls being 0.6 metres in width. They are now mainly grass-covered. The chapel was excavated by the Rev. F. Hancock in 1897. Before then the ruin had been quarried as a source of stone. Little is known about the chapel, but it was described as St. Andrew's Chapel in a document of 1776. Hancock thought that it was St. Saviour's Chapel dating to

1316.

Reading. Chadwyck Healey 1901, 24,104.

Nearby sites. 73 Horner; 81 Joaney How and Robin How; 120 Selworthy; 148 West Luccombe.

29 CHARD MUSEUM

Location ST 319 086. The museum is situated on the west side of Chard. Godworthy House, High Street, Chard.

Parking. There is roadside parking in Helliers Road (the first turning northwards past the museum), and limited parking outside the museum.

Access for disabled visitors. There is parking outside the museum, and level access to the archaeological displays on the ground floor, apart from one step at the museum entrance. There is a toilet for the disabled only.

Admission charge. There is an admission charge, and an annual subscription can be bought.

Open. Early May to mid October, Monday-Saturday, 10.30am-4.30pm; also Sundays in July and August.

The Museum. The museum was opened in 1970 and is run by volunteers. The collections are mainly local history and bygones, but there are a few archaeological finds including Palaeolithic handaxes, a Bronze Age cremation urn found near Perry Street in 1855, Roman artefacts, and a model and maps of Chard in the Medieval period.

Nearby sites. 27 Castle Neroche; 117 Robin Hood's Butts; 136 Taunton; 153 Witcombe.

Charlton Musgrove, see **Stavordale Priory**.

30 CHARTERHOUSE-ON-MENDIP,
Blackmoor Nature Reserve (Roman lead mining site and associated fort, prehistoric enclosure)

Location and parking ST 504 556. Five kilometres north-east of Cheddar. Take the minor road south-westwards off the B3134 at ST 508 568 and a crossroads is just over one kilometre. Turn left on to the minor road at the crossroads (the west turn goes to Shipham). Behind the trees in a field on the left, the slight earthworks of a square Roman fort are visible at ST 504 557.

At the end of the road is the Blackmoor Nature Reserve's car park. Take the footpath to the left, which leads past an earthwork enclosure (poss-

Carved Roman gemstones from Charterhouse-on-Mendip.

ibly prehistoric) on the right-hand side, overgrown with gorse and scrub. Keep to the established paths as there are dangerous mine shafts, unstable ground and deep ponds. Return to the car park, then walk up the southwards path where deep trenches (rakes) are visible on the hilltop at ST 507 553.

Access for disabled visitors. The Roman fort earthworks are visible from the road. The rest of the site is inaccessible, but the disturbed ground caused by later lead mining activity is clearly visible from the car park.

Site description. Charterhouse, established around AD 48, was the earliest and most important Roman lead mining site in Britain, and was initially under military control. It continued to operate up to the 4th century. The lead ore was mined, the silver was removed, and the remaining lead was cast into oblong ingots known as pigs. Much of the lead was exported, and a cistern found at Pompeii, Italy, (a town destroyed in AD 79) has been shown to be made from British (probably Charterhouse) lead. The lead ingots were often inscribed with information such as the emperor's name, date, and the authority in control of the mines. A Roman fort was constructed, probably for guarding the mines, and an associated

settlement grew up nearby with a small amphitheatre to provide entertainment. The mining and processing of lead ore may have continued during the Dark Ages. Activity is certainly documented during the Medieval period, from the 12th century onwards. It reached a peak in the 17th century, and continued to the present century. Much of the 19th century workings survive, and at this time earlier waste was extensively reworked. The waste heaps are contaminated by lead and zinc, and a wide area is now the Blackmoor Nature Reserve, largely owned by Somerset County Council. Because of subsequent intense industrial activity, little of the Roman lead works survives, but was probably in the area of the deep rakes.

Reading. Budge et al 1974; Burnham & Wacher 1990, 208-11; Wilson 1988, 100-2.

Nearby sites. 31, 32, 33 Charterhouse-on-Mendip; 86 Lord's Lot.

31 CHARTERHOUSE-ON-MENDIP
(Roman amphitheatre)

Location ST 498 565. 4.5 kilometres north-east of Cheddar. Take the minor road south-westwards off the B3134 road at ST 508 568, and a turning to the radio masts is on the right after a distance of nearly one kilometre. Go up this no-through road (Rains Batch), and the earthworks of the amphitheatre are visible in the field on the left.

Parking. There is limited roadside parking, with more room to park near the radio masts.

Access for disabled visitors. The site is visible from the road.

Site description. The substantial earthworks of an elliptical-shaped enclosure are the remains of a Roman amphitheatre associated with the nearby settlement for the lead mines. The amphitheatre was surveyed and excavated in 1909. Its arena measures 32 metres x 24.4 metres, and the banks for the seating survive 4.5 metres above the arena floor. There are two opposing entrances on the east and the west.

Reading. Budge et al 1974; Burnham & Wacher 1990, 209-11; Burrow 1924, 105 (figure); Gray 1910.

Nearby sites. 9 Beacon Batch; 30, 32, 33 Charterhouse-on-Mendip.

32 CHARTERHOUSE-ON-MENDIP
(Medieval enclosure)

Location ST 501 560. 4.5 kilometres north-east of Cheddar. Take the minor road south-westwards off the B3134 road at ST 508 568, and the site is in a field on the right after a distance of one kilometre. It is a rectangular enclosure, 150 metres south-west of the road which leads up to the radio masts.

Parking. There is limited roadside parking.

Access for disabled visitors. The site can be viewed from the road.

Site description. The enclosure is marked by a fairly conspicuous rectangular embankment. It is possibly of Medieval date.

Reading. Budge et al 1974.

Nearby sites. 9 Beacon Batch; 30, 31, 33 Charterhouse-on-Mendip.

Cheddar, concrete pillars marking the posts of the halls of the Saxon palace.

33 CHARTERHOUSE-ON-MENDIP
(Medieval enclosure)

Location ST 501 564. 4.5 kilometres north-east of Cheddar. Take the minor road south-westwards off the B3134 road at ST 508 568, and a turning to the radio masts is on the right after a distance of nearly one kilometre. Go up this no-through road (Rains Batch), and on the right-hand side by an iron stile where the stone wall stops, there is a low earthwork at ST 501 564. A footpath goes from the stile across one edge of the earthworks.

Parking. Limited roadside parking is possible.

Access for disabled visitors. The site is visible from the road.

Site description. This small, sub-rectangular enclosure has an entrance on its south-west corner. Excavation has shown that it is possibly of Medieval date.

Reading. Budge et al 1974.

Nearby sites. 9 Beacon Batch; 30, 31, 32 Charterhouse-on-Mendip.

34 CHEDDAR (Saxon and Medieval palace site and Medieval chapel)

Location ST 457 531. In Cheddar village, on the west side of the B3135 (Axbridge to Cheddar Gorge) road, in the grounds of the Kings of Wessex Community School, adjacent to the school's car park.

Parking. In the school's visitors' car park.

Access for disabled visitors. A good view of the palace site and the chapel can be obtained from the surrounding level paths by the car park. Access inside the chapel is possible across a fairly level grassed area.

Facilities. There is an information board by the site. There are toilets just outside the school entrance, and the village has shops, refreshments and banks.

Site description. This was the site of successive Saxon and Medieval palaces, known through documentary sources, and excavated for a total of ten months in 1960-62 in advance of the construction of the present school. The remains were considered so important that the position of the school buildings was moved (to an area largely unexcavated!) to enable the main buildings to be laid out for display: the postholes of the West Halls and East Halls are marked by concrete blocks set in a grassed area. The adjacent chapel of St. Columbanus is now a conserved ruin.

A Roman villa existed in this area about 220 metres distant, near St. Andrew's Church, but nothing is now visible. Meetings of the

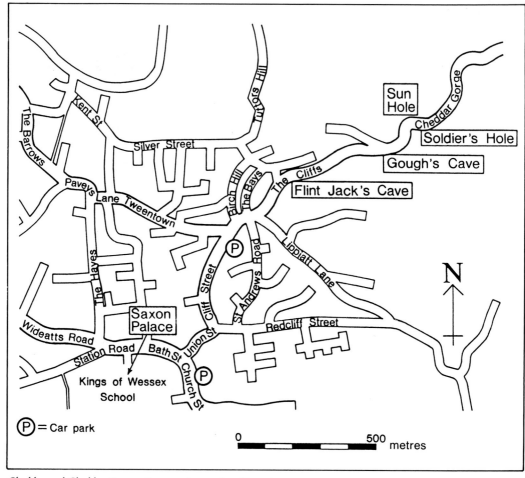

Cheddar and Cheddar Gorge - Saxon palace and position of caves.

witenagemot (royal court) are recorded in three charters at Cheddar for 941, 956 and 968, and so a palace must have existed then. Archaeological excavation showed that the first Saxon settlement dated to the 9th century or earlier, the main building consisting of a Long Hall orientated north-south. After about 930 another hall was built (West Hall I), and a chapel (Chapel I) was constructed over the Long Hall. There is no documentary reference to Cheddar between 968 and the Norman Conquest, but archaeological evidence shows that it was occupied: in the late 10th-11th century, the west hall and chapel were rebuilt (West Hall II, Chapel II).

By the time of the Domesday Book (1086), the royal estate had been divided into four manors, with forest rights being retained by the king. The settlement may still have been a royal residence, and in the later 11th-12th century, the west hall was rebuilt (West Hall III) and a very large east hall was constructed (East Hall I). This east hall was rebuilt in the early 13th century (East Hall II).

In the later 13th century the site had passed into episcopal hands and the chapel which still stands today was completely rebuilt. There is documentary evidence that the chapel was dedicated to St. Columbanus by 1321, and considerable modifications were made to the chapel at this time. What is visible today are the remains of a 13th and 14th century chapel. By about 1400 the east and west halls had been abandoned, and there were cottages on the site. After the Reformation in the 17th century, the chapel was converted to domestic occupation and possibly a barn. In about 1800 it was divided into two cottages, but around 1910 the roof was stripped off. The chapel became derelict, and much of it collapsed.

Reading. Rahtz 1979; Rahtz & Hirst 1987.

Nearby sites. 5 Axbridge; 13 Black Down; 35 Cheddar Gorge; 139 Tyning's Farm.

35 CHEDDAR GORGE (Palaeolithic caves, and museum)

Location ST 466 538. Cheddar Gorge runs north-east from Cheddar village, and is the route of the B3135 road. The caves are at the lower end of the gorge. Walking from the village, Gough's Cave is on the right, and by the entrance to this cave is a museum. These are run by Cheddar Showcaves, Cheddar Gorge, BS27 3QF, tel. Cheddar (0934) 742343. The National Trust owns almost the whole of the north side of the gorge.

Flint Jack's Cave is at ST 463 538, 15 metres above the road, Gough's Cave is at ST 467 539, Sun Hole is at ST 467 541, and Soldier's Hole is at ST 468 539, 183 metres east of and 30 metres above Gough's Cave.

Parking. There is a large pay car park in Cliff Street by the village at the foot of the gorge (opposite Gordons Hotel), and several car parks at the other end of the gorge, the furthest ones being free-of-charge. Free roadside parking is possible in the winter season.

Access for disabled visitors. None, but the exterior of the caves can be viewed from the road.

Facilities. Refreshments and shops are available in the gorge. There are toilets by the museum and elsewhere in the gorge.

Admission charge. The tourist attractions can be visited singly, or a single overall ticket can be purchased.

Open. The show caves and museum are open every day Easter to September, 10am to 5.30pm, and October to Easter 10.30am to 4.30pm.

Site description. Caves and shelters in Cheddar Gorge were used during the end of the last glaciation in Britain (12,000-9000 BC), including Flint Jack's Cave, Gough's (New) Cave, Great Oone's Hole and Soldier's Hole, all on the south side of the gorge. On the north side of the gorge is Sun Hole Cave, and another cave used at this period once existed in Chelm's Combe Quarry, 500 metres to the north-west, but it was destroyed in 1964. Gough's Cave is the richest Upper Palaeolithic site in Britain, and in 1903 a skeleton of a young adult male ('Cheddar Man') was discovered, dating to the Mesolithic period, later in date than the main use of the cave for occupation. Excavations again took place from 1927, and over 7000 pieces of flint and chert were found, as well as bone and antler artefacts, and animal bones. Finds of later date have also been found in other caves in the gorge.

The museum is of particular archaeological interest. There are finds from Gough's Cave, including a cast of the skeleton of 'Cheddar Man'. Finds and photographs of all periods from the general gorge area are on display, and also reconstruction models of the Cheddar Saxon palace, the Charterhouse Roman lead mines, and a travelling bronzesmith dating to around 1000 BC (Bronze Age). There is also a large reconstruction model of Cheddar Man and companions living in a cave, complete with sound effects.

Reading. Jacobi 1982a; Jacobi 1982b.

Nearby sites. 5 Axbridge: 13 Black Down; 34 Cheddar; 139 Tyning's Farm.

Chilcompton, see **Blacker's Hill**.

36 CLANVILLE (Medieval ridge-and-furrow)

Location ST 620 328. 0.75 kilometres north-west of Castle Cary. Ridge-and-furrow can be seen in the field on the north side of the B3153 road just west of the railway bridge, near a white gate leading to Clanville Manor.

Parking. There is limited roadside parking.

Access for disabled visitors. Easily visible from the roadside but parking is limited.

Site description. The ridge-and-furrow here is particularly pronounced and is part of the extensive Medieval field system in this area. Ridge-and-furrow can be seen in fields along the whole stretch of the B3153 road from Clanville to East Lydford, but is not always well-defined. The best view is from a train on the Taunton to Castle Cary line.

Reading. Whitfield 1981 (Medieval field systems in south-east Somerset).

Nearby sites. 20 Bruton; 26 Castle Cary; 55, 56 East Lydford.

37 CLATWORTHY CAMP (Iron Age hillfort)

Location ST 044 314. Five kilometres north-west of Wiveliscombe. The hillfort is situated on a promontory of the Brendon Hills above Clatworthy Reservoir. Much of it is inaccessible, but part of the ramparts are within land belonging to Wessex Water and are on the route of a nature trail. Follow the signposts to Clatworthy Reservoir, and the entrance to the visitors' car park is by a pair of houses at ST 041 308. The pay car park is 300 metres further north along the track. Take the permitted path downhill through the perimeter fence and across the dam. Go round to the right, and then left into the woods (signposted to the nature trail) just before a large gate with a 'no public access' sign. Follow the footpath uphill, and as it turns left, the hillfort rampart can be seen. Further along the path, the rampart and ditch become much more prominent, running parallel to the path on the right-hand (north) side. Further on there is an entrance through the rampart and ditch at the west end of the hillfort on the right-hand side, and the path then turns left away from the hillfort.

Access for disabled visitors. None.

Facilities. There are toilets and a picnic area in the car park.

Open. The car park is open daily 8am to sunset.

Site description. Clatworthy Camp or Castle is an Iron Age hillfort defended by a single bank and ditch enclosing a roughly triangular area of 5.8 hectares. The ditch is cut through solid rock, and there may have been an entrance on the west and two entrances on the east. The hillfort was heavily wooded earlier this century, but much has since been cleared. It overlooks the valley of the River Tone, now flooded as Clatworthy Reservoir.

Reading. Burrow 1924, 78, 79 (figure); Burrow 1981, 212-13.

Nearby sites. 59 Elworthy Barrows; 75 Huish Champflower Barrow; 114, 115 Ralegh's Cross.

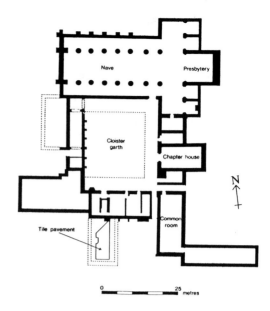

Plan of Cleeve Abbey.

38 CLEEVE ABBEY, Washford (Medieval abbey)

Location and parking ST 046 407. Situated in Washford, 250 metres south of the A39 road, along a minor road to Roadwater. A large car park is on the west of this road at ST 045 407, from which there is a three-minute walk to the abbey on the east of the road. Tel. Washford (0984) 40377.

Access for disabled visitors. Access is possible in the grounds and on the ground floor, with car parking in the abbey grounds near the ticket office.

Facilities. There are toilets and a sales area.

Admission charge. There is a charge (English Heritage).

Open. Open all year: 10am-6pm summer season, 10am-4pm winter, closed 24-26 December and 1 January.

Site description. The remains of this Cistercian abbey are situated in peaceful surroundings. It was founded in the very late 12th century (about 1198) for Cistercian monks by William, Earl of Roumare, and was dedicated to the Blessed Virgin. The monastery prospered throughout the 13th century, and by 1297 there were 26 monks. It began to decline during the 14th century, although matters did improve during the later 15th century. The monastery was dissolved in 1537, and the church

Cleeve Abbey, view of the cloisters.

Cleeve Abbey, part of the tiled frater floor.

was probably demolished soon after. The remaining abbey buildings and lands passed through several hands, and then in the late 19th century George Luttrell of Dunster purchased the ruins of the old abbey which were being used as farm buildings. He repaired the buildings and began excavations of other buildings, including the church. In 1951 the site passed into the care of the Ministry of Works (now English Heritage).

Only the foundations of the monastic church survive, but many of the buildings around the cloister still stand, including the 13th century east range with its first-floor dorter, and the 15th century south range with the first-floor frater containing a fine timber roof. The tiled floor belongs to the earlier 13th century frater, and there are 13th and 15th century wall paintings. There is also a gatehouse, the upper storey of which was rebuilt by the last abbot in the early 16th century. A later farmhouse adjoins the south-west corner of the cloister. Recent restoration has enabled more of the buildings to be opened to the public, and displays include two realistic life-size models of monks.

Reading. Gilyard Beer 1960; Scott Holmes 1911, 115-18.

Nearby sites. 7 Battlegore; 44 Daw's Castle; 64 Gallox Hill; 142 Watchet.

39 COAT (Medieval ridge-and-furrow)

Location ST 456 206. 0.5 kilometres north-west of Martock. The ridge-and-furrow is situated to the east of Coat, in the first field to the east of the line of the old railway, south of the road from Coat to Stapleton Cross. It is visible from the field gate.

Parking. There is limited roadside parking.

Access for disabled visitors. The ridge-and-furrow can be viewed from the field gate.

Site description. The ridge-and-furrow in this field is quite distinct and represents a surviving portion of the Medieval field system in this area.

Reading. Whitfield 1981 (Medieval field systems in south-east Somerset).

Nearby sites. 25 Cart Gate; 48 Drayton; 72 Ham Hill; 128 Stoke-sub-Hamdon.

Cockercombe Camp, see **Plainsfield Camp.**

40 COUNTY GATE (Bronze Age round barrows and standing stones)

Location and parking SS 798 483. 8.5 kilometres WNW of Porlock. On the south side of the A39 road on the Devon/Somerset border, there is a car park at SS 793 486 from where two standing stones are visible on the crest of the hill to the south-east. Cross the road to the trackway signposted 'Bridleway Culbone'. After 50 metres, turn right (south) onto a faint path uphill across the heather moor. Towards the top of the hill, there are two low mounds (Bronze Age round barrows) either side of the path about 50 metres apart. 50 metres further on there are two standing stones about 30 metres apart on either side of the path. Allow ten minutes to walk from the car park to the standing stones.

Access for disabled visitors. There are toilets at the car park. The monument is inaccessible, but the best view of the standing stones is from a parking area near the road to Yenworthy Lodge at SS 801 481.

Facilities. There are toilets at the car park, as well as a large Exmoor National Park Authority information centre and shop, open 10am-5pm.

Site description. The two Bronze Age barrows are only 0.3 metres in height; a very low mound between them may indicate the position of a third barrow. They may be contemporary with the two nearby standing stones. The two stones are each about one metre in height.

Reading. Fowler 1988, 9; Grinsell 1969, 37.

Nearby sites. 43 Culbone Hill; 87 Madacombe; 107 Porlock Common; 151 Whit Stones.

41 COW CASTLE (Iron Age hillfort)

Location and parking SS 793 373. 5.75 kilometres WSW of Exford. The hillfort can be approached from Simonsbath, on a recommended Exmoor National Park walk. It is quite wet and boggy in places and suitable footwear is recommended. Park in the Ashcombe car park at SS 774 395, which is reached from a lane 50 metres south-west of the church and is signposted. Walk back up the lane to the road and turn right, passing on the right the Exmoor Forest Hotel and Pound Cottage (a single-storey building). Cross the road here, and to the left of a trackway is a small wooden gate with a signpost to Wheal Eliza, Cow Castle, Landacre and Withypool. Go through the gate into the woodland, and just inside is a signpost. Take the route signposted to 'Landacre via Cow Castle 5'. Continue along the path through the woodland and out into more open ground along the river valley, following the yellow waymark signs and the pairs of posts. After nearly one kilometre there is a small gate, the other side of which a stream has to be crossed. After a further 400 metres the path bears left and goes across open flat ground, rejoining the river after 150 metres. The path then goes past the ruins of Wheal Eliza cottage where mining once took place. Continue along the path by the river for just over a kilometre, and Cow Castle is on the hill in front. The path goes up the steep side of the hillfort, and the circuit of the ramparts can be walked. Allow a total of 2½ hours to and from Simonsbath along this route.

Access for disabled visitors. None.

Facilities. There are toilets in the Simonsbath car park and refreshments in the village. A picnic area is adjacent to the car park.

Site description. Cow Castle is an Iron Age hillfort and occupies an isolated sandstone hilltop, defended by a single rampart and ditch enclosing 0.9 hectares. It is within a steep-sided valley of the River Barle with higher moorland all round. There are entrances on the south-west and north-east.

Local legend relates that the hillfort was built by fairies to protect themselves against the earth-spirits.

Reading. Burrow 1924, 78, 79 (figure); Burrow 1981, 243; Grinsell 1970, 85-6; Grinsell 1976a, 99.

Nearby sites. 15 Blue Gate; 71 Green Barrow and Brightworthy Barrows; 138 Two Barrows; 141 Wambarrows.

42 CROWCOMBE (Medieval crosses and Church House)

Location and parking ST 140 366. One cross is in the churchyard near the porch of the Church of the Holy Ghost. The market cross is west of the church in the main street, nearly opposite the Carew Arms. There is a car park next to Church House, which is situated opposite the church.

Access for disabled visitors. The churchyard can be entered using the sloping tarmac path, and the market cross and Church House are on the roadside.

Site description. The Church House was built in the local red sandstone as a parish hall in 1515 for church ales and other fund-raising activities, and is the only surviving example of such a building in modern-day Somerset. It underwent various subsequent uses such as a poorhouse, reading room and army canteen, but in 1977 the whole building reverted to use as a parish hall. In the churchyard to the south of the church is a 14th century cross with sculptured figures on the shaft which have been identified as a bishop, St. John the Baptist and possibly a prioress of Studley. The shaft is set in a square socket on three octagonal steps. Part of the upper section of the original 14th century 24.5 metre spire of the church stands in the churchyard east of the church. It was brought down by lightning in 1725, causing much damage. Inside the church are fine examples of carved oak bench ends of 16th century date. Just west of the church is the original 14th century market cross.

Reading. Bush 1985, 63; Pooley 1877, 183-5.

Nearby sites. 45 Dead Woman's Ditch; 47 Dowsborough; 105 Plainsfield Camp; 137 Trendle Ring.

Crowcombe, Medieval churchyard cross.

Crowcombe, market cross.

Culbone, Dark Age inscribed stone.

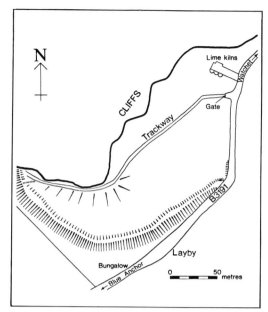

Plan of Daw's Castle.

43 CULBONE HILL (Dark Age inscribed stone)

Location and parking SS 832 473. Five kilometres west of Porlock. Take the turning north-eastwards off the A39 road opposite the Culbone Inn. The turning is signposted to Yarner Farm. After 90 metres there is a large car parking area just beyond the cattle grid on the left side of the road. Alongside there is a stile with a signpost to 'Culbone Stone'. Cross the stile and go along the path, turning left into the dwarf conifer plantation at the next sign. The stone is at the end of this worn path. It is a three-minute walk from the car park to the stone.

Access for disabled visitors. None.

Site description. The inscribed memorial stone has a ring-cross motif (a cross in a circle with a stem), and is about 0.6 metres in height. It was re-erected in 1940 on the spot where it was discovered lying face down. The stone may have been re-used from a nearby prehistoric stone row (not accessible to the public). It probably dates to the 7th-9th century.

Reading. Eardley-Wilmot 1988, 33-4; Fowler 1989, 9; Grinsell 1970, 106.

Nearby sites. 40 County Gate; 87 Madacombe; 107 Porlock Common; 151 Whit Stones.

44 DAW'S CASTLE , Watchet (Saxon burh)

Location and parking ST 061 431.
0.75 kilometres west of Watchet. Take the B3191 road westwards from Watchet to Blue Anchor. The road bends round to the left and then to the right, and a layby is on the left-hand (south) side, with a steep drop to the valley below, overlooking the paper mill. Walk back round the bend (2-minute walk), and on the left-hand (west) side is a metalled trackway with padlocked gates, and a stile. Go over the stile, and walk along the well-worn path, which at one point runs quite close to the cliff edge. 180 metres west of the stile, the path goes across the ramparts, and then advances downhill to a field boundary by the 'dangerous cliff' sign. There is a well-worn path round the ramparts to the south, but the rampart earthworks are only discernible on the west side, although the ground does fall sharply away to the road in the rest of the field.

Access for disabled visitors. The position of the site can be viewed from the layby, but very little can be seen.

Site description. Daw's Castle is situated on the edge of Lias cliffs. Earlier this century these cliffs were eroding rapidly with the loss of hundreds of tons of red sandstone each year, but now they are much more stable. The name 'Daw's Castle' derives from Thomas Dawe who owned a field called 'le castell' around 1537. It has also been called 'Dart's Castle' and 'Dane's Castle'. It appears to be the site of a burh or fort recorded at Watchet in the Burghal Hidage in the early 10th century, and was possibly built by King Alfred. Excavations have shown that the defences consisted of an insubstantial mortared wall 0.85 metres wide and 0.6 metres high, with a bank behind about seven metres wide. Later on, the defences were altered, and a larger mortared wall was constructed, 1.44 metres wide. A bank was built up behind it, and in front there was a ditch 1.5 metres wide. This second system of defences seems to have been undertaken in the late 10th or early 11th century, probably for additional protection against Scandinavian raids.

At present the monument covers about two hectares, but much is likely to have been lost by coastal erosion. On the west and south-west sides (close to a bungalow) the earthwork of the bank can be seen up to two metres high, but it is less clear further east. On the east side, the road to Watchet may have cut through the defences which are likely to have continued into the field east of the road. The ramparts once extended up to the cliffs on the east side of the 19th century limekilns. These ramparts were visible earlier this century, but have since been destroyed through cliff erosion. On the west of the site, an east-west rampart was also visible on the edge of the cliffs, but this has also gone. When the lime workings were constructed in the 19th century, many human bones were found, possibly from part of a Saxon cemetery belonging to a minster: the field to the east was known as 'Old Minster' in 1801.

According to the Anglo-Saxon Chronicle, raiders at Watchet were beaten off in 914, but further raids took place in 988 when 'Watchet was ravaged', and in 996 raiders landed at Watchet and 'wrought great havoc by burning and killing people'. A coin mint was established at the burh in about 980, but no coins were struck by Watchet from 1056 to 1080: Daw's Castle may have already been abandoned, the inhabitants possibly moving to the site of the present town. In the past, Daw's Castle has been used as a golf course and as a council rubbish tip, but it is now owned by the Department of the

Environment and is in the care of English Heritage.

Reading. Burrow 1924, 140, 141 (figure); Burrow 1981, 86-7, 191 plan Bb, 232; McAvoy 1986.

Nearby sites. 7 Battlegore; 38 Cleeve Abbey; 64 Gallox Hill; 142 Watchet.

45 DEAD WOMAN'S DITCH
(Linear earthwork)

Location and parking ST 161 382 to ST 161 380. Three kilometres south-west of Nether Stowey. A fairly large car park is adjacent to the site at the intersection of the road from Nether Stowey to Crowcombe with a road which leads from the A39 road. The earthwork extends southwards to the forest plantation, and it can be seen in places in the woodland to the north of the road.

Dead Woman's Ditch and Dowsborough Hillfort. Dead Woman's Ditch extends further north and south, but has never been surveyed.

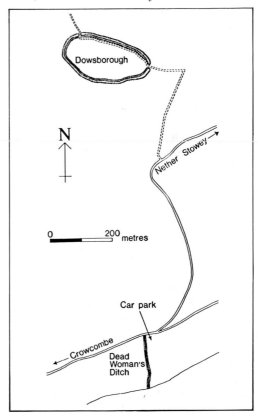

Access for disabled visitors. From the car park there is a fairly rough but level track running southwards alongside the earthwork.

Site description. Dead Woman's Ditch consists of a quite pronounced linear rampart up to 1.7 metres high with a ditch on the west side. It is covered in trees. The visible part of this earthwork extends southwards over 200 metres from the road to the forest. Part of the forest has been recently cleared, and the earthwork can be seen running southwards down the valley. Grinsell has recorded that it extends as far south as Rams Combe valley, and as far north as Lady's Combe valley. Parts of the earthwork can be seen close to the road in the woodland to the north of the road. The earthwork may have been an Iron Age boundary connected with Dowsborough hillfort to the north.

The site is said to be so-called because of the murder of a young woman called Jenny. In the late 18th century she used to visit John Walford in his charcoal burner's hut. After her second child by him, he was forced to marry her on June 18th 1789, but on July 5th he murdered her and dumped her body in the prehistoric ditch. He was subsequently hanged on the common (marked by the name 'Walford's Gibbet' nearby at ST 175 394). However, Grinsell has shown that the site was called Dead Woman's Ditch before this event, as it was shown as such on Day and Masters' Map of Somerset of 1782.

Reading. Grinsell 1976b, 19-20; Hurley 1982, 11-12.

Nearby sites. 42 Crowcombe; 47 Dowsborough; 101 Nether Stowey; 105 Plainsfield Camp.

Deer Leap, see **Ramspits**.
Deer Leap Stones, see **Ebbor**.

46 DOWNEND (Medieval castle)

Location ST 309 413. Four kilometres north of Bridgwater off the A38 Bristol Road. Turn east into Downend Road, and the site is in the adjacent pasture field.

Parking. There is limited parking by the field just off the A38 road by Downend Road.

Access for disabled visitors. The site is visible from the roadside.

Site description. The modern hamlet of Downend can be identified as the Medieval borough of Caput Montis which was probably in existence before 1159 when it is first mentioned in a document of that date. It may have been established as a port to take advantage of the traffic on the nearby River Parrett and the east-west traffic along

Plan of Downend Castle.

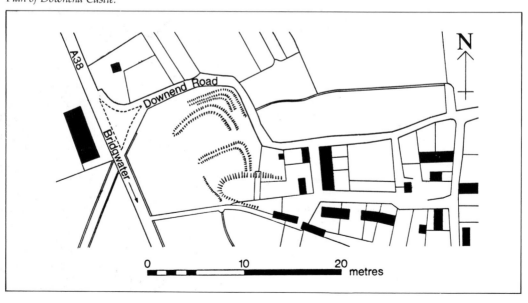

the Polden ridgeway. There is no mention of the borough in later Medieval documents, so as a planned town it presumably failed. It had a castle which was probably Norman in date, and was situated at the extreme end of the Polden Hills ridge. It was constructed by contouring the natural shape of the hill to form a motte. Excavations took place in 1908: 'August 3. Four men were employed for the work, -all used to digging the soil of the locality, and all natives except the foreman, who was sexton of the parish but foreign-born (Stogursey)' (Chater & Major 1910, 163).

In one corner of the field the motte can be seen, and in the rest of the field there are the embankments of the two baileys of this small castle. The field was once known as 'Bally Field'.

Reading. Aston & Leech 1977, 39-40, maps 16, 17; Burrow 1924, 124, 125 (figure); Chater & Major 1910.

Nearby sites. 18, 19 Bridgwater; 62 Fiddington; 125 Spaxton.

47 DOWSBOROUGH (Iron Age hillfort)

Location and parking ST 160 391. 2.5 kilometres SSE of Nether Stowey. There is a car park by Dead Woman's Ditch (ST 161 381) at the intersection of the road from Nether Stowey to Crowcombe and another road. Walk along the northern road for 650 metres, and just beyond the bend turn left (north) along the well-worn but unmarked bridleway. Follow this path through the woodland for 275 metres to the junction with an east-west path. Turn left (west), and after 100 metres the path crosses over the hillfort ramparts at the original hillfort entrance. The path then follows the line of a substantial bank and ditch.

Access for disabled visitors. None, and the hillfort is not visible from a distance as it is obscured by woodland.

Site description. Dowsborough (also called Danesborough or Dawesbury) is a small Iron Age univallate hillfort, roughly oval in shape, and enclosing about 2.5 hectares. It is largely covered in trees and scrub, but a substantial rampart is still visible, surviving up to four metres in height above an outer ditch. The main entrance is on the east, and an entrance on the north side may also be original. A possible Bronze Age round barrow at the western end of the hillfort is not visible

amongst the vegetation.

Reading. Burrow 1924, 80, 81 (figure); Burrow 1981, 226-7.

Nearby sites. 42 Crowcombe; 45 Dead Woman's Ditch; 101 Nether Stowey; 105 Plainsfield Camp.

48 DRAYTON (Medieval cross)

Location ST 405 247. 2.25 kilometres south-west of Langport. The cross is in the churchyard, by the south porch of the parish church of St. Catherine.

Access for disabled visitors. The entrance to the churchyard is on the south-east.

Site description. The 14th century cross has three octagonal steps, a square socket, and a square shaft with a sculpture on the south face. There is a spherical head, which Pooley describes as 'a debased successor to its proper head'. The worn sculpture represents St. Michael with a sword and shield conquering the Dragon.

Reading. Pooley 1877, 187.

Nearby sites. 25 Cart Gate; 39 Coat; 98, 99 Muchelney.

Drayton churchyard cross.

49 DUNKERY BEACON (Bronze Age round barrows)

Location and parking SS 891 415. Five kilometres south of Porlock. There is a car park along the east side of the road from Chapel Cross to Dunkery Gate at SS 903 419. From the car park, walk along the road (northwards) for a short distance, and there is a very worn path on the left (west) leading south-westwards to Dunkery Beacon. It is signposted 'Dunkery Beacon 1'. After a distance of 100 metres, the Kit Barrows should be visible on the crest of the hill to the right, but they are obscured by the vegetation.

Dunkery Beacon can also be reached from Great Rowbarrow to the west, a distance of 1.5 kilometres along a well-worn path.

Access for disabled visitors. None.

Site description. Dunkery Beacon is the highest point of Exmoor (519 metres OD) and is part of the National Trust's Dunkery estate. Bronze Age round barrows are sited on many of the Exmoor ridges, and it is likely that a similar cluster of stone-built barrows (cairns) existed here. However, the use of this ridge as a fire beacon over the centuries, and the constant artificial piling up of stones have obscured the archaeological features. On the very top of the hill there is a concrete cairn commemorating the gift of Dunkery to the National Trust in 1935, built on a huge mass of stones, probably once the site of a Bronze Age cairn. Just to the south-east there is a small cairn, probably the only visible survivor of several Bronze Age barrows.

Reading. Grinsell 1969, 30; Grinsell 1970, 154.

Nearby sites. 28 Chapel Cross; 70 Great Rowbarrow and Little Rowbarrow; 81 Joaney How and Robin How; 131 Sweetworthy.

Dunster , see also **Bat's Castle, Black Ball Camp, Gallox Hill.**

50 DUNSTER (Medieval castle)

Location and parking SS 991 434. The castle is in the care of the National Trust: Dunster Castle near Minehead, Somerset, TA24 6SL. Tel. Dunster (0643) 821314. At Dunster go past the Yarn Market, and at the traffic lights do not follow the road to the right, but go straight ahead up the narrow roadway (Castle Hill) and turn left to the car park. Alternatively, turn off the A39 road into The Drive which leads directly to the car park.

If coming from the direction of Timberscombe, turn right into the alternative National Trust entrance before the town centre is reached, opposite Chapel House and St. Georges Street. Turn left into the car park. There is a charge for the car park, except for National Trust members.

Walk to the stables (housing the National Trust shop) and up the steep slope to the gatehouse. Go through the single arched gatehouse, and on the right, adjoining the gatehouse (signposted 'Castle Entrance'), is the 13th century gateway flanked on each side by a tower. Climb up the steps through the gateway and at the top is a lawn and gardens ('Green Court') which was the bailey or lower ward. Beyond it is a large mound ('the Tor'), originally the castle motte.

Turn right along the path, and on the right-hand side at the edge of the gardens is the 'Ruin' which is the remains of a tower. Continue along this path and take one of the paths leading up the motte as far as a large flat area.

Access for disabled visitors. There is access up the very steep tarmac slope only as far as the gatehouse. However, on days when the house is open, go to the attendant at the main car park. From here you will be given access to drive up to the house where there is parking by 'Green Court' and from where the ruined round tower and the motte can be visited. The ground floor of the house is also accessible. Any necessary companion for a disabled person who requires physical support (not just wheelchair users) is admitted free-of-charge. A Batricar is also available for use by disabled people free-of-charge: go to the attendant at the main car park. There are toilets at the top of Castle Hill opposite the stables.

Facilities. There are toilets near the stables, and a shop in the stables. Refreshments, shops and banks are in the town. Picnics can be had in the park.

Admission charge. A charge is made, except to National Trust members. A ticket for the garden and grounds only will be adequate for visiting all the original elements of the Medieval castle.

Open. The house is open 25 March to 30 September 11am-5pm except Thursday and

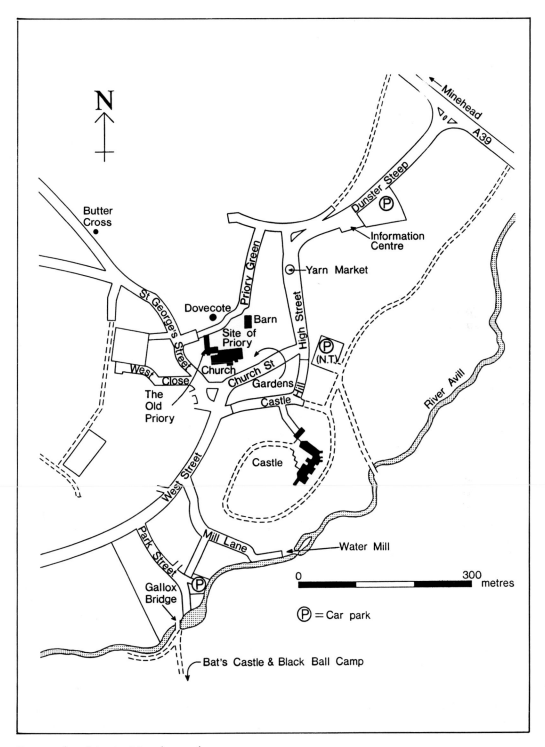

N

Butter
Cross

Minehead

A39

Dunster Steep

Information
Centre

Yarn Market

St George's Street

Priory Green

High Street

Dovecote

Barn

Site of
Priory

Church

Church St

West
Close

Gardens

Castle Hill

The
Old
Priory

Castle

River Avill

West Street

Park Street

Mill Lane

Water Mill

Gallox
Bridge

0   300
                metres

℗ = Car park

Bat's Castle & Black Ball Camp

Dunster, plan of sites to visit and car parks.

Dunster, the ruined castle tower.

Friday; also 1 October-3 November 12pm-4pm except Thursday and Friday.

The garden and grounds are open 1 March-3 November 11am-5pm (or dusk if earlier) every day.

Site description. The castle is sited on a steep natural hill or Tor. The existence of a castle is recorded in Domesday when a site known as the 'Torre' (later Dunestorre, and then Dunster) is mentioned which is probably Castle Hill. After the Norman conquest, Dunster was granted to William de Mohun. No sign of the Norman castle survives but it probably consisted of earthwork defences and timber buildings. However, documentary sources do relate much of the later history of the site. William de Mohun II (who died around 1155) built stone fortifications in the 12th century, but the oldest surviving part of the castle is the 13th century gateway with its original oak doors. This was built by Sir Reynold de Mohun II, and led into the lower ward (now known as Green Court). The gateway is flanked on either side by a semi-circular tower, the upper parts of which have long been demolished. The lower ward or bailey was a crescent-shaped area which originally sloped upwards from the gateway to the Tor. Sir Reynold surrounded the lower ward by a curtain wall with D-shaped towers and the gateway. Part of the lower section of the curtain wall survives on the north side of Green Court, above which rises a single 13th century D-shaped tower, renovated in the 18th century. In 1764 a level court was created on the site of the lower ward. The upper ward or keep was on top of the Tor, the summit of which was artificially levelled, and was probably surrounded by a stone wall like that of the lower ward.

In 1376 Lady Joan de Mohun sold Dunster to Lady Elizabeth Luttrell whose descendants continued to own the site until the present century. In the early 15th century Sir Hugh Luttrell undertook extensive repairs and built the gatehouse (which

Dunster Castle, the Gatehouse or Barbican.

was probably at the entrance to a barbican). The heraldic panel over the gatehouse entrance was set up in the early 16th century by his descendant Sir Hugh Luttrell. By the mid 16th century Leland describes the castle as being in a state of disrepair, and in 1617 George Luttrell commissioned William Arnold to build a new mansion in the lower ward. This house incorporated parts of the Medieval buildings, and has undergone subsequent extensive alteration and refurbishment, in particular by Anthony Salvin from 1867 onwards. In the Civil War, the castle was a Royalist stronghold, and so in 1650 an order was made for it to be demolished, but shortly afterwards George Luttrell was allowed to take up residence after paying a fine. Early in the 18th century, the upper ward on top of the Tor was levelled and made into a bowling green.

In 1976 the castle and thirty acres of the surrounding park were presented to the National Trust by Lt.-Colonel Walter Luttrell.

Reading. Aston & Leech 1977, 46, map 20; Gibbs 1981; National Trust 1987.
Nearby sites. 51, 52, 53, 54 Dunster.

51 DUNSTER, Butter Cross (Medieval cross)

Location SS 987 438. The cross is situated on the north-west side of Dunster. Go up St. Georges Street, directly opposite the west entrance to Dunster Castle and by the side of Chapel Cross. There is an English Heritage sign to Butter Cross. After 350 metres, just beyond the last house on the right which is called 'Butter Cross', there is a raised green on the right. At this point a bridlepath and public footpath converge. The cross is on the raised green, and is in the care of English Heritage.

Parking. There is limited parking by the green, or alternatively the cross is only a short walk from Dunster centre.

Access for disabled visitors. The cross is accessible, with adjacent parking.

Facilities. Shops, banks, toilets and refreshments are available in Dunster.

Site description. The Medieval wayside cross is called the 'Butter Cross'. It consists of two octagonal steps, a square socket and a shaft fragment one metre in height. It is 15th century in date, and may have once stood in the High Street.

Reading. Pooley 1877, 154.
Nearby sites. 50,52, 53, 54 Dunster.

52 DUNSTER (Medieval priory & cross)

Location and parking SS 990 436. Take the turning southwards to Dunster off the A39 road, and park on the left in Dunster Steep pay car park. (There is parking in the High Street, but it is usually congested). Walk along Dunster Steep to the town centre, down the length of the High Street and then turn right into Church Street. On the right is a red sandstone building hung with grey slates known as the Nunnery. Go on past a high wall, at the end of which is an archway with wrought iron gates, opposite the public toilets. Go through the archway into the Village Gardens, adjacent to the church. Walk across the gardens and through the smaller archway opposite into a large walled garden, now laid mainly to lawn. The gardens were part of the priory and were later

Dunster, the monastic dovecote.

dens. It is advisable to enter the church through the churchyard entrance with the lychgate at the junction of Priory Green and St. Georges Street. There are toilets in the Dunster Steep car park.

Facilities. There are toilets in the Dunster Steep car park and in Church Street (opposite the Village Gardens). Refreshments, shops and banks are situated in the town.

Site description. The Nunnery was never a nunnery, but was previously called High House. However, it is a good example of a timber-framed and red sandstone Medieval building, partly obscured by the later slate cladding.

The Benedictine priory at Dunster was a cell of Bath priory, established in the early 12th century, and was never a large foundation. At that time a church (dedicated to St. George) was constructed, with the priory to the north. Bath Priory undertook much of Dunster's administration until the appointment of Robert de Sutton as prior in 1332. Then the priory began to manage more of its own affairs, and had a prior and four monks.

The L-shaped building adjoining the west end of the church, and now known as The Old Priory, is probably all that remains of the original priory. This part is likely to have been used as the refectory and as offices. From this building a cloister ran along the north side of the church (now the Garden of Remembrance) and further east were the kitchen gardens.

A little to the north-west is the prior's tithe barn, a large 16th century building with old doors and massive door jambs. To the west was the prior's dovecote, probably of 13th or 14th century date. It was actually a pigeon breeding house, circular in shape, with a height of 8.5 metres and an internal diameter of 4.5 metres. Inside may still be seen the revolving ladders which were used for cleaning out the nests, collecting eggs and taking young birds from their nests. The dovecote could hold around 2000 birds. It has been recently restored, and an information board is sited nearby.

The parish church of St. George was built by the priory not long after the Norman Conquest, possibly on the site of an existing church, and parts of this Norman church are still visible. The church continued to be enlarged and altered, particularly in the 15th century when much rebuilding took place. The eastern part of the church

used as kitchen gardens for the castle. Diagonally opposite is another archway with a wrought iron gate.

Go through the archway, and on the right is the monastic tithe barn. Across the road (Priory Green) is the circular dovecote of the priory.

Opposite the dovecote an entrance leads into the Garden of Remembrance (once the cloisters) on the north side of the church. Adjoining the west side of the church is a house called The Old Priory, which was part of the monastic buildings, and is also visible from the churchyard. The church can be entered through the north door. Alternatively, continue down Priory Green to the junction with St. Georges Street. Go through the lychgate into the churchyard from where The Old Priory can be seen and also the remains of an old cross in the churchyard. Enter the church by the south door.

Access for disabled visitors. The easiest access is to park in Priory Green near the dovecote, from where the dovecote and tithe barn are visible. Access can be obtained from here to the Village Gar-

Dunster, Gallox Bridge.

was used by the monks, and the western part or nave by the parishioners. Owing to disputes, the immense rood screen was erected as a physical barrier to separate the two parts of the church. After the Dissolution, it was normal for the eastern part of such churches to be demolished, but Dunster is a rare example of where it was allowed to remain. The priory church did become extremely neglected and partly ruinous by the mid 19th century, but was subsequently restored and preserved by the Luttrell family. It now consists of a nave with north and south aisles, tower, north and south transepts, and a chancel with chapels on the north and south sides. There are many fine Medieval monuments, some very ornate.

The cross in the churchyard has three circular steps, a circular socket, and a portion of shaft. It dates to the late 13th century.

The priory was included in the surrender of the priory of Bath to the Crown on 27 January 1539. In about 1540 Leland wrote 'the late Priory of Blake Monkes stoode yn the Rootes of the North West side of the Castelle and was a celle to Bathe. The hole Chirch of the late Priory servith now for the Paroche Chirch. Afore tymes the Monkes had the Est Parte closid up to their Use'. Much of the priory land was leased to John Luttrell of Dunster (the brother of Sir Andrew, then owner of Dunster). In 1557 Thomas Luttrell succeeded to Dunster Castle on the death of his elder brother, Sir John, and shortly afterwards much of the priory appears to have been demolished, the rest being converted to a farmhouse (now called The Old Priory).

Reading. Hancock 1905; Pooley 1877, 154; Scott Holmes 1911, 81-2.

Nearby sites. 50,51,53, 54 Dunster.

53 DUNSTER, Gallox Bridge (Medieval bridge)

Location and parking SS 989 432. In West Street, turn south into Park Street (signposted to the Water Mill and Gallox Bridge) by the Foresters Arms and the telephone kiosk. There is a pay car park at the bottom of this road by Mill Gardens. From the car park, turn left to the bridge by the thatched cottages (two-minute walk).

Access for disabled visitors. Parking is possible right by the bridge, and there is level access to the bridge.

Facilities. Shops, refreshments, banks and toilets are available in the town.

Site description. Gallox Bridge is a Medieval

bridge with two ribbed arches crossing the River Avill. There is a cutwater on the upstream side only. It was originally called 'Doddebridge', and was used for packhorses, while carts drawn by horses or oxen used the adjacent ford. It has a roadway width of nearly one metre. The bridge is 10.5 metres in length and 1.2 metres wide. Just over the bridge, beyond the thatched cottages, several trackways converge (including the old coach road), and it was here that a gallows once stood, giving the bridge its present name. The bridge is in the care of English Heritage.

Reading. de Maré 1954, 120; Jervoise 1930, 114, pl. 66.

Nearby sites. 50,51,52,54 Dunster.

54 DUNSTER, Visitor Centre

Location and parking SS 992 438. Take the turning southwards to Dunster off the A39 road, and a pay car park is on the left in Dunster Steep. The visitor centre is adjacent to the car park. Exmoor National Park Visitor Centre, Dunster Steep, Dunster. Tel. Dunster (0643) 821835.

Access for disabled visitors. Access is possible to most of the visitor centre. Toilets are in the car park.

Facilities. Refreshments are nearby and in the town, as well as shops and banks. A picnic area is adjacent to the car park.

Open. March to mid-November 10am-5pm daily; also Christmas.

Site description. The visitor centre is the Exmoor National Park information centre. There is a huge panorama from a painting portraying Dunster High Street market as it might have been on 11 May 1500, which gives a good idea of the appearance of the castle and village of that time. There is also a display on the contemporary woollen industry.

Nearby sites. 50,51,52,53 Dunster.

55 EAST LYDFORD
(Medieval ridge-and-furrow)

Location ST 577 309. Six kilometres WSW of Castle Cary. Ridge-and-furrow can be seen in the field to the south of the B3153 road, opposite New Manor Farm, 1.25 kilometres east of the Lydford-

on-Fosse crossroads.

Parking. There is limited roadside parking.

Access for disabled visitors. Visible from the roadside, but parking is limited.

Site description. The ridge-and-furrow here is particularly pronounced and is part of the Medieval field system in this area. Ridge-and-furrow can be seen in fields along the whole stretch of the B3135 road, from East Lydford to Clanville, but is not always well-defined. The best view is from a train on the Taunton to Castle Cary line.

Reading. Whitfield 1981 (Medieval field systems in south-east Somerset).

Nearby sites. 26 Castle Cary; 36 Clanville; 56 East Lydford; 147 West Camel.

56 EAST LYDFORD (Medieval church ruins)

Location and parking ST 575 317. 6.5 kilometres west of Castle Cary. From the B3153 road 700 metres east of the Lydford-on-Fosse crossroads, turn northwards into Church Lane. After 600 metres, the road turns sharply left: at this point take the turning which is straight ahead. This no-through road becomes a track, at the end of which are three farm gates. Parking is possible here if the gates are not in use. Two public footpaths are signposted – take the one which goes straight ahead over the ditch and stile. The church ruins are just west of the footpath, 80 metres from the stile, visible as a fenced area about 20 metres x 20 metres, covered in trees and scrub. There is a sign on the fence 'Site of old church 1311-1866'.

Access for disabled visitors. The site can be viewed from the area of the farm gates.

Site description. The Medieval church of St. Peter was situated at the northern end of the village street near the River Brue. It is known from 19th century watercolours to have been a small stone building with a chancel and nave, a small square bell turret housing two bells on the west gable end, and a large south porch. Documentary sources suggest that it may once have had a tower. Due to its proximity to the river, the church was periodically flooded. It is known that a wall was swept away in a great flood in 1786, and in 1799 the church had to be cleaned after another

Ebbor, Deer Leap Stones.

flood. In 1864 the parishioners decided to rebuild the church on a new site as the old one was dilapidated, damp and inconvenient. Now only masonry walls, tombstone fragments and other debris from this former church are visible.

From the old church, a long stretch of the Roman road (Fosse Way), now a busy road, can be seen, and the Church of the Blessed Virgin Mary, which was built 500 metres to the south-west in 1864, is also visible. This church was built in a 14th century style, nearer the centre of the village and can be reached from a little gateway and path off Church Lane. It is now redundant and in a state of dereliction, and appears to be about to suffer the same fate as its predecessor.

Reading. Bush 1974, 128 and figure showing watercolour of the church in 1833.

Nearby sites. 26 Castle Cary; 36 Clanville; 55 East Lydford; 106 Ponter's Ball Dyke.

57 EBBOR, Deer Leap Stones
(Prehistoric standing stones)

Location and parking ST 517 487. Four kilometres north-west of Wells. The site is alongside the road from Priddy to Wookey Hole and is best approached from Priddy. This is largely a single-track road, and so parking is difficult, but there is a car park further south on the left-hand (east) side of the road at Ebbor Gorge (ST 521 482). Walk back up the road 500 metres to a footpath sign next to a stile opposite a passing place. The stones can be seen from the footpath near the road in the northern corner of the field.

Access for disabled visitors. The stones can be seen from the field gate by the road at the top of the field, fifty metres north-west of the footpath. Parking is difficult as the road is single track.

Site description. Two quartzite standing stones about 1.2 metres high are situated sixteen metres apart. Until 1964 they stood east of a drystone wall field boundary which was dismantled in that year for building stone. At the same time the workmen were stopped from destroying the standing stones, and the farmer replaced the southern one with a similar stone from an old nearby quarry. He also raised the northern stone from a semi-recumbent to an upright position. The origin of the stones is not known but they may be of Bronze Age date. A similar stone once existed in a wall (destroyed in 1968) 200 metres to the north, but these two Deer Leap stones were never incorporated in any field boundary. There was a local legend that the stones commemorated a phenomenal leap by a deer.

Reading. Stanton 1981.

Nearby sites. 58 Ebbor Gorge; 109 Priddy; 116 Ramspits; 158 Wookey Hole.

Ebbor Gorge.

58 EBBOR GORGE

(Area of prehistoric caves)

Location and parking ST 521 485. 3.5 kilometres north-west of Wells. The site is on the single track road from Wookey Hole to Priddy. It is more easily approached from Priddy. There is a fairly large parking area (not signposted) on the east side of the road. From the car park, follow the route near the information centre. Go down the steep path with the steps, and up the gorge following the longer (red waymarked) nature trail – a distance of about three kilometres. In the gorge, rock shelters and fissures are visible, but are mostly obscured by vegetation. This part of the walk is steep, rough and slippery in places. After passing through the gorge, follow the signs to the car park, shortly after which there is a sign 'Danger Cliff Edge'. From this point there are fine views of the gorge. Return to the path and continue to follow the signs back to the car park. Allow at least one hour; suitable footwear is advised. Public rights of way also criss-cross the nature reserve.

Access for disabled visitors. There is a viewpoint in the car park extension which overlooks the gorge, where there is a commemorative plaque noting the gift of the site.

Facilities. There is a picnic area and an information board. Leaflets are usually available to buy for a nominal sum.

Site description. Ebbor Gorge is a National Nature Reserve managed by English Nature and leased from the National Trust (to whom it was presented in 1967 by Mrs GW Hodgkinson in memory of Sir Winston Churchill).

The nature reserve consists of Hope Wood (nearest the road) and Ebbor Wood which covers the limestone cliffs and gorge of Ebbor Rocks. The site is only one kilometre from the caves of Wookey Hole, and many caves and rock shelters are known, of which 26 have been named. Some of the caves were used in the Upper Palaeolithic right up to the Roman period. Caves are situated in the gorge and closer to the car park in Primrose Valley, but are largely obscured by vegetation.

The best-known caves are Bracelet Cave (also known as Hope Wood Cave) in which Bronze Age, Iron Age and Roman deposits were found, including nine skeletons. It is situated at ST 523 483 high up at the south-east end of the cliffs above the nature trail, on the south side of Primrose Valley. Cook's Hill Hole has produced Bronze Age, Iron Age and Roman pottery as well as a crouched skeleton (found in 1950). It is situated at ST 522 485 high up at the north-west end of the cliffs above the nature trail, on the south side of Primrose Valley. Outlook Cave is on the west side of the gorge at ST 525 487 and contained human bones and Neolithic pottery. Beaker Shelter (at ST 526 486) also yielded evidence of Neolithic and Beaker occupation. At Bridged Pot Shelter (at ST 526 486) there is evidence for Upper Palaeolithic occupation, as well as Neolithic and Beaker finds.

Reading. Barrington & Stanton 1976; McBurney 1959, 262-5, pl. XVIII.

Nearby sites. 57 Ebbor; 109 Priddy; 116 Ramspits; 158 Wookey Hole.

Elworthy Barrows, aerial view (photo by M. Aston).

59 ELWORTHY BARROWS
(Iron Age hillfort)

Location ST 070 337. Six kilometres NNW of Wiveliscombe. The road from Elworthy Cross to Ralegh's Cross climbs fairly steeply. After nearly two kilometres, the hillfort is visible on the left (south) side of the road from the third field gate beyond the minor road on the south. A radio mast is situated in the field.

Parking. The road is fairly wide enabling roadside parking.

Access for disabled visitors. The site is visible from the road by the field gate.

Site description. Elworthy Barrows (or Burrows) appears to be an unfinished Iron Age hillfort, oval in shape, and covering 2.9 hectares. The circuit of the uneven unfinished ramparts survives intermittently, but much of it is in a reasonable condition. A ditch is visible in places, and there is an inturned entrance on the east. Despite being called Elworthy Barrows, no Bronze Age round barrows are known on the site, but the unfinished ramparts may have resembled such barrows, thereby giving the site its name.

Reading. Burrow 1924, 106, 107 (figure); Burrow 1981, 222-3.

Nearby sites. 37 Clatworthy Camp; 75 Huish Champflower Barrow; 114, 115 Ralegh's Cross.

60 FARLEIGH HUNGERFORD
(Medieval castle)

Location ST 801 576. Five kilometres west of Trowbridge, Wiltshire. The castle is situated on the north side of the A366 road, on a slope overlooking the River Frome. From the direction of Somerset, turn east off the A36 road on to the A366 road. The castle is on the left after a distance of 1.5 kilometres.

Parking. A car park for visitors is reached through the castle gateway.

Access for disabled visitors. There is partial

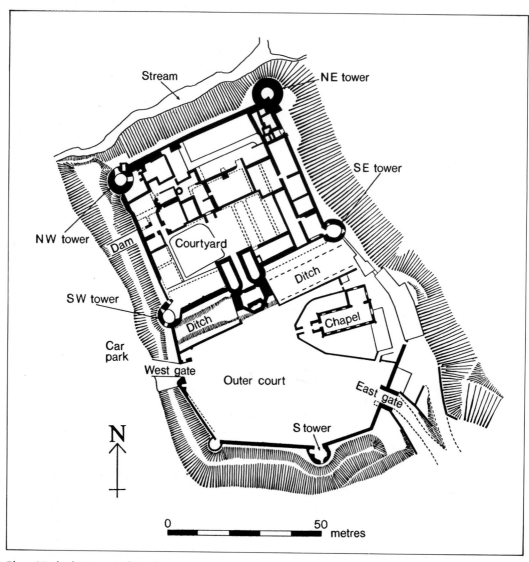

Plan of Farleigh Hungerford Castle.

access to the exterior only from the car park and
along the main path to the ticket office, with a
mixture of gravel paths and uneven crazy paving.
It is possible to look down into the Priest's House
(steps lead down into the building) and to go
round the path (narrow in places) to the chapel
entrance (steps lead down into the building).

Facilities. There is a sales area and toilets.

Admission charge. In the care of English
Heritage. Admission is charged.

Open. All year: 10am-6pm daily 1 April to 30
September, 10am-4pm Tuesday to Sunday 1 Oc-
tober to 31 March. Closed 24-26 December and 1
January.

Site description. In the late 14th century the
Norman manor house known as Farleigh Montfort
was fortified by Sir Thomas Hungerford, speaker
of the House of Commons. He died here in 1397,
and is buried in a massive tomb-chest in St.
Leonard's Chapel. The castle was extended by his

Farleigh Hungerford Castle.

son Sir Walter around 1420-30 by the addition of the outer court. He was also Speaker and fought at Agincourt. During the Wars of the Roses the family supported the Lancastrians, and in 1462 Richard, Duke of Gloucester, acquired the castle. When he became King in 1483, it was granted to the Duke of Norfolk, but he died on Bosworth Field in 1485 and the Hungerfords regained the property in 1486. In 1522 the property was left to Agnes Hungerford but she was hanged at Tyburn in 1523 on a charge of having murdered her first husband at Farleigh Castle. Her son Walter Hungerford was executed in 1540 for treason and unnatural vice, and the castle was confiscated by the king for the second time. It was granted to Sir Thomas Seymour, but he in turn was executed in 1549. Queen Mary sold the castle back to the Hungerfords in 1554. The castle was sold in 1686 by Sir Edward Hungerford 'The Spendthrift' and by 1701 it was in a ruinous state. In 1915 it was placed in the guardianship of the Ministry of Works by Lord Cairns, and is now in the care of English Heritage.

The castle was protected by ditches (mainly dry) and by the natural escarpment. The main entrance (originally with a ditch and drawbridge) was by the East Gate, but little survives of the West Gate.

The chapel of St. Leonard dates from the mid 14th century and was originally the parish church. It has wall paintings, probably dating from the 14th century. Beneath the chapel the crypt contains lead coffins, of 16th and 17th century date.

The Inner Court was the original 14th century castle, consisting of a rectangular enclosure surrounded by a curtain wall with a circular tower at each corner. Parts of the curtain wall survive, and the south-west and south-east towers are still standing, but all buildings of the Inner Court were destroyed in the 18th century, leaving only the foundations visible. Writing around 1540, Leland said 'There be diverse praty Towrres in the utter Warde of the Castelle'.

The Priest's House formerly housed a display of armour, but the collection is currently in store and undergoing conservation at the Tower of London. Upstairs in the Priest's House is an exhibition of photographs and finds relating to the site, and a model of the castle.

Reading. *Farleigh Hungerford Castle* booklet produced by English Heritage (no author cited); Wilcox 1980.

Nearby sites. 63 Frome; 84 Kingsdown Camp; 90 Marston; 119 Rowley.

61 FENNY CASTLE (Medieval castle)

Location ST 508 436. 4.5 kilometres south-west of Wells. The castle is situated on Castle Hill, and can be reached from rather narrow roads leading south from the B3139 road between Worth and Wookey at ST 514 453, which goes past Castle Farm and Fenny Castle House.

The castle is in a field separated from the road by a deep wide rhyne (drainage ditch). A good view of the castle can also be obtained from the minor road from Polsham to Fenny (at ST 512 435).

Parking. There is very limited roadside parking near the gate from which the earthworks are visible.

Access for disabled visitors. The castle can be viewed from the field gate by the road.

Site description. Fenny is an impressive motte and bailey castle consisting of a large natural mound, surrounded by earthworks and rising twenty metres above the flat North Moor. A few trees grow on top and on the sides of the motte. The site has the appearance of two mottes, but this is because of the natural shape of the hill and the ditch which was cut across it to form a motte, with part of the hill becoming the bailey. Quarrying has also disturbed the appearance of the site. Leland in about 1540 observed masonry ruins on the site which are no longer visible. The Rev. John Skinner excavated the site in 1825. The history of the castle can be traced back to the 14th century, but local tradition says that it is the burial place of King Alfred.

Reading. Bothamley 1911, 529.

Nearby sites. 68 Glastonbury; 145, 146 Wells; 158 Wookey Hole.

62 FIDDINGTON (Sheila-na-gig, Medieval cross)

Location ST 216 405. Eight kilometres north-west of Bridgwater. Take the turning northwards off the A39 road at ST 219 393, signposted to Fiddington. The Sheila-na-gig is carved on the exterior south wall of the nave of the parish church. It is 2.8 metres above ground level, more than halfway up the nave wall, and to the east of the porch. It is situated at the south-east corner of the nave, at its junction with the chancel, which is

The sheila-na-gig on Fiddington church.

set back from the nave. It lies to the west of the chancel window and is between two nearby down-pipes. It is difficult to see, as it is now much obscured by lichen.

Parking. There is room to park by the village hall.

Access for disabled visitors. Parking outside the church is possible, but access through the churchyard may be difficult. The path, of stone chippings, is only about 0.3 metres wide and is flanked by grassy slopes. The path is bumpy but fairly level.

Site description. Sheila-na-gigs are commonly found in Ireland, but there are very few in England and Wales. In Somerset there are two on roof bosses of the west cloister of Wells Cathedral and one at Fiddington. They are mainly dated to the 11th-12th century, but their nature and purpose are much disputed. They are female fertility figures with exaggerated genitalia, and are one type of the blatant sexual figures often found in churches dating to the Medieval period. They may represent pagan fertility beliefs adopted by the Christian church, or they may have been intended to deter devils and perpetrators of evil.

The Fiddington figure is 0.3 metres high. The upper part of the figure is well carved, but the lower part appears to have suffered damage in the past, possibly deliberate in order to erase the erotic

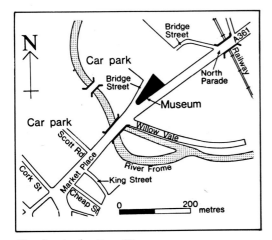

Plan showing location of Frome museum.

nature of the carving.

Nearly opposite the carving in the churchyard is the remains of a Medieval (early 14th century) cross shaft on three steps and a socket. The steps are now circular but were probably once octagonal. There is carving on the east side of the shaft, but the cross is very worn. Inside the church are carved bench ends dating to around 1500. The church is kept locked, but details of how to obtain the key are on the porch door.

Reading. Aston 1979; Pooley 1877, 132.

Nearby sites. 101 Nether Stowey; 125 Spaxton; 127 Stogursey; 152 Wick Barrow.

63 FROME (Museum)

Location ST 778 481. In the Literary Institute, 1st floor, 1 North Parade, Frome.

Parking. There is a pay car park nearby, adjacent to the Cattle Market.

Access for disabled visitors. None.

Facilities. There is a sales area and toilets; refreshments and banks are available in the town.

Admission charge. A small charge is made.

Open. Wednesday to Saturday 10am-4pm (or by special arrangement for parties).

The Museum. The museum is run by volunteers. It moved to its present location in 1987 and is still expanding. It incorporates a display of some archaeological finds and photographs of sites relating to Frome and the district. There are also displays on history, geology and bygones.

Nearby sites. 84 Kingsdown Camp; 90 Marston; 92 Marston Moat; 103 Nunney Castle.

Gallox Bridge, see **Dunster.**

64 GALLOX HILL (Linear earthwork)

Location SS 990 420. 1.5 kilometres south of Dunster. This earthwork is 125 metres south-east of Bat's Castle, and is easily visited on the same trip. From Bat's Castle, continue south-eastwards along the path until it passes through a single rampart and ditch. On the left (north) of the path, the rampart turns a right-angle, parallel with the path, and then turns northwards again. On the right of the path, the earthwork runs in a southerly direction until it meets woodland.

Parking. There is a pay car park at Mill Gardens in Dunster near the Gallox Bridge.

Access for disabled visitors. None.

Facilities. There are toilets, refreshments, shops and banks in Dunster.

Site description. The linear earthwork on Gallox Hill consists of a bank of stones and a shallow ditch. It takes a zig-zag course across the ridge in an approximately south-west to north-east direction, and is 180 metres long. It was originally thought to be a Civil War defence, but is now believed to be a defence associated with the nearby Bat's Castle hillfort, and is therefore probably Iron Age in date.

Reading. Burrow 1981, 242.

Nearby sites. 8 Bat's Castle; 12 Black Ball Camp; 50, 53 Dunster.

65 GLASTONBURY
(Saxon and Medieval monastery)

Location ST 501 387. The abbey is approached through the gatehouse off Magdalene Street, near the garage. For further details, contact the Custodian, The Abbey Gatehouse, Glastonbury. Tel. Glastonbury (0458) 32267.

Parking. There is a pay car park at the rear of the garage in Magdalene Street, or there are more distant car parks in the town.

Access for disabled visitors. Access is possible to much of the ruins, and there are also toilets.

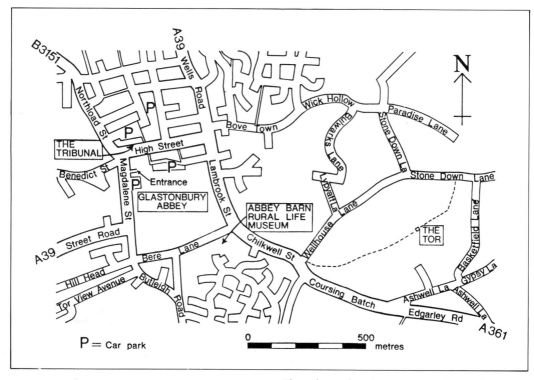

0   500
                               metres

Glastonbury, plan of sites to visit and car parks.

Facilities. There are male and disabled people toilets only (female public toilets are by the garage). There is a shop. The site consists of 36 acres, with a picnic area. There are plans to construct a new visitor centre, museum, and toilets.

Admission charge. Admission is charged.

Open. All year except 25 December, 9.30am-6pm (or dusk if earlier). Open from 9am in June, July and August.

Site description. It is uncertain when the first religious community at Glastonbury was founded, but through the *Anglo-Saxon Chronicle* it is known that King Ine (688-725) built a church here. A later account by William of Malmesbury, writing in the 12th century, says that the abbey was founded in 601, before the Saxon conquest of Somerset. As yet there is no evidence to substantiate this, and a later date seems more likely. Little is known about the site until Dunstan became abbot (940-956); he was responsible for much rebuilding, for establishing Glastonbury as an important monastery, and introducing the Benedictine rule. The abbey be-

Cup found in the ruins of Glastonbury Abbey, said to be made of wood from the flowering thorn.

Glastonbury Abbey, the ruined church.

The lead cross supposed to have been found with the burial of King Arthur at Glastonbury.

came increasingly prestigious, and three Saxon kings (Edmund, Edgar and Edmund Ironside) were buried here, along with a multitude of saints. By the Norman Conquest, Glastonbury was one of the wealthiest Benedictine abbeys in the country, and owned one-eighth of all Somerset.

Throughout the Medieval period, Glastonbury was the wealthiest monastery in England, and was responsible for the shaping of areas of the Somerset landscape, especially in the Levels which it began to drain. In May 1184 a devastating fire destroyed most of the abbey's buildings, treasures and manuscripts.

Many legends surround the site, a large number dating back to the Medieval period. One of the best-known concerns the burial of King Arthur. In 1191, just after the fire, the monks claimed to have found the bodies of King Arthur and Queen Guinevere who died in the 6th century. This apparently miraculous discovery gave the monks suitable relics with which to attract pilgrims and much-needed income to rebuild the monastery. Found with Arthur's burial was a leaden cross,

Glastonbury Abbey, the Lady Chapel with the Romanesque north door.

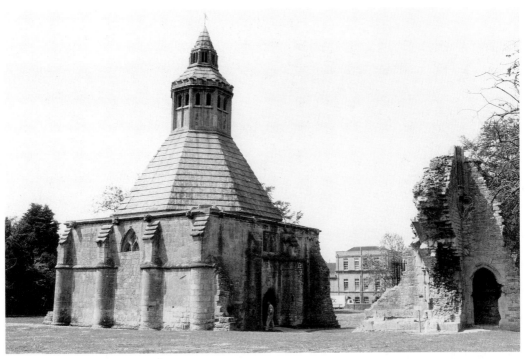

Glastonbury Abbey, the Abbot's Kitchen.

which has since disappeared, but a drawing shows lettering which is probably 12th century in style, and it is generally thought that the discovery of the bodies was an elaborate hoax in order to increase revenue after the fire.

Massive rebuilding took place from the very end of the 12th century, more or less continuing until the early 16th century. In 1539 the abbey was dissolved after the execution of the abbot on Glastonbury Tor. In 1559 the site was granted to Sir Peter Carew, and the church and many other buildings in the precinct began to be used as a quarry by the townspeople.

In 1723 William Stukely visited Glastonbury, and devoted several pages of his *Itinerarium Curiosum* to the abbey. Much more damage was done at the end of the 18th century and beginning of the 19th century when John Down, mayor of Glastonbury and a local brickmaker, used gunpowder in his quarrying operations on the site. During the 19th century, there was a revival of interest in the abbey site, and the destruction was halted in 1907 when the site was purchased for the Church of England. Thirty-four seasons of excavation took

place from 1904 to 1964; these excavations remain all but unpublished (see Aston & Leech 1977, 57-8, 59, map 24 for a full list).

There is much for the visitor to see despite the neglect and destruction of the centuries, particularly the remains of the abbey church and the 15th century abbot's kitchen. The most complete building is the Lady Chapel which was built just after the 1184 fire. In the town of Glastonbury and the surrounding area, there are many other buildings associated with the abbey and its estates. These include the George Inn or Pilgrim Inn in the High Street (which was built in the 15th century by Abbot John Selwood and was used as lodgings by pilgrims), the fish house at Meare, and the tithe barn at Doulting.

Reading. Abrams & Carley (eds) 1991; Aston & Leech 1977, 57-65; Carley 1988 (well-illustrated and detailed historical account, including information on the legends, early chroniclers, the abbey library, and post-Dissolution history); Foster 1987 (on Anglo-Saxon sculptured stones); Scott Holmes 1911, 82-99; Taylor & Taylor 1965, 250-7.

Nearby sites. 66, 67, 68, 69 Glastonbury.

Glastonbury Abbey Barn (Somerset Rural Life Museum).

66 GLASTONBURY (Medieval priory barn)

Location ST 503 385. The barn is situated at the junction of Chilkwell Street and Bere Lane by the mini-roundabout on the east side of Glastonbury. It houses a Somerset County Council museum: Somerset Rural Life Museum, Abbey Farm, Chilkwell Street, Glastonbury, BA6 8DB. Tel. Glastonbury (0458) 31197.

Parking. A large car park lies to the rear of the barn, and a coach layby on the road in front.

Access for disabled visitors. Access to the barn is possible and there are also toilets.

Facilities. A picnic area is at the rear of the barn. There are also toilets and a shop. A tea room is open April to September. Other facilities are available in the town.

Admission charge. Admission is charged. Free to Friends of the Abbey Barn and members of the Somerset Archaeological and Natural History Society.

Open. Easter to 31 October: weekdays 10am-5pm, weekends 2pm-6pm; 1st November to Easter: weekdays 10am-5pm, Saturday 11am-4pm, apart from 25 and 26 December and 1 January.

Site description. This late Medieval stone barn was originally part of the abbey, and was situated to the south-east outside the abbey precincts. It was probably constructed in the 14th century, with a thatched roof being replaced by stone tiles later on in the 14th century. It has a fine raised base-cruck roof, and measures internally 25.85 metres x 7.85 metres, this area being divided into seven bays.

The museum contains artefacts, reconstructions and displays relating to the more recent agricultural and rural history of Somerset.

Reading. Bond 1988; Bond & Weller 1991; Bridge & Dunning 1981.

Nearby sites. 65, 67, 68, 69 Glastonbury.

Glastonbury Tribunal.

67 GLASTONBURY TRIBUNAL
(Museum and Medieval building)

Location ST 499 389. Glastonbury Tribunal is in the High Street.

Parking. There are pay car parks in the town and limited parking on the opposite side of the High Street.

Access for disabled visitors. The ground floor is level, but there are two steps at the entrance. Parking is possible in the High Street opposite the Tribunal.

Facilities. There is a small sales area. Shops, refreshments, banks and toilets are available in the town.

Admission charge. In the care of English Heritage. Admission is charged

Open. All year, daily in summer 10am-6pm, and in winter Tuesday to Sunday 10am-4pm. Closed for lunch 1-2pm, and 24-26 December and 1 January.

Site description. The two-storey L-shaped building was once thought to be the courthouse ('tribunal') of Glastonbury Abbey. The existing building dates to about 1400, and the present facade was added during the time of Abbot Bere around 1500, replacing a half-timbered facade,

when the whole building may have been reconstructed. The name 'tribunal' was probably first used in 1791, and the building was actually always a Medieval domestic merchant's house, the only surviving substantial building of its kind in Glastonbury.

The Tribunal is used as a museum, and the finds are largely the responsibility of the Glastonbury Antiquarian Society. They include the exceptional Iron Age finds from the Glastonbury Lake Village. There is also a model of the lake village, and a wooden canoe dug up nearby by Arthur Bulleid on Crannel Moor. One end of the canoe was uncovered by a man when cleaning out a ditch, and he had it brought to the attention of Bulleid some eight years later. Some Medieval and later finds from the town and the Tor are also on display.

Reading. Bulleid 1893, 121 (on the discovery of the canoe); Dunning 1991; Pantin 1964, 217.

Nearby sites. 65, 66, 68, 69 Glastonbury.

68 GLASTONBURY, Lake Village (Iron Age settlement)

Location ST 493 407. 1.5 kilometres NNW of Glastonbury. The site is on the east side of the road from Godney to the B3151 road, in the angle of a junction with another minor road. It is in a pasture field, and can be viewed from a white field gate.

Parking. There is very limited roadside parking.

Access for disabled visitors. The site is visible from the field gate by the road.

Site description. The only visible remains of this exceptional lake village site are minor earthworks in the field. The so-called lake village site was never situated in open water, but was constructed on marshy land at the edge of what was probably the original course of the River Brue. It consisted of a massive platform made from felled trees, stones and brushwood. During its lifetime there were up to eighty timber huts on this platform, built on thick clay floors, with wattle and daub walls and raised hearths. The roofs were probably thatched. The whole settlement was surrounded by a timber palisade.

The site dates from about 300 BC in the Iron Age and probably continued to be occupied into the early Roman period (around AD 100), when it was abandoned, possibly due to a rise in the water level.

Discoveries at the site were first made in the years following 1834, and Arthur Bulleid undertook large-scale excavations from 1893 to 1907. Because the site had remained waterlogged within the Somerset Levels since the Iron Age, a wealth of well-preserved objects and structures was discovered, such as wooden bowls, ladles and ladders, and the remains of wooden posts, floors and walls. Such finds are not normally discovered on archaeological sites, as they would have long since perished. Other finds included highly decorated pottery, glass beads, and bone and antler objects. Many finds are on display in the Glastonbury Tribunal, including a model of the 'lake village'.

Reading. Bulleid & Gray 1911; Coles, B&J 1986; Coles, B&J 1989, 39-40, 140-4.

Nearby sites. 65, 66, 67, 69 Glastonbury.

69 GLASTONBURY TOR
(Medieval church tower)

Location and parking. ST 512 386. One kilometre south-east of Glastonbury town centre. Take the A361 road out of Glastonbury (a south-east direction from the roundabout near the Rural Life Museum). Then turn left (north) into Wellhouse Lane, where there is a fairly steep footpath just on the right which leads to the Tor summit. There is roadside parking near the Rural Life Museum for this route. A shorter route is to continue along Wellhouse Lane to the north side of the Tor where there is a small layby for parking, and from where a steep footpath and steps lead to the Tor summit.

Access for disabled visitors. None, but the Tor is visible from a distance. The closest viewpoint is from the layby on the north side of the Tor.

Site description. The poet Thomas Shoel described it in 1818 as:

Of look so pleasing and of conic height;
That proudly tow'rs above the lowly plains,
And o'er the neighb'ring hills conspicuous reigns'

Glastonbury Tor is in the care of the National Trust. It consists of a church tower on top of a prominent natural oval hill which rises to 158 metres OD and from where there are extensive views. Terracing is visible on the sides of the hill, which are probably Medieval strip lynchets making use of this higher ground for cultivation.

From excavations there is evidence for Dark Age occupation on the site from the 6th century, and also later Saxon occupation. A monastery of St. Michael of Torre existed on the site in the early Medieval period, and probably came under the control of Glastonbury Abbey. Its church was destroyed by an earthquake in 1275. The surviving church tower on the summit of the hill is 14th century in date, with 15th century additions, and is the only remaining part of the second church of St. Michael. The church and other buildings on the Tor probably ceased to function at the time of the dissolution of Glastonbury Abbey in 1539, when Richard Whiting, the last Abbot of Glastonbury Abbey, and two of his monks were hanged on the Tor on 15th November 1539. The church became ruined, but the tower was restored in the late 18th century. A great deal of myth and legend is now associated with the Tor.

Reading. *Glastonbury Tor* leaflet produced by the National Trust; Rahtz 1968.

Nearby sites. 65, 66, 67 Glastonbury; 106 Ponter's Ball Dyke.

70 GREAT ROWBARROW and LITTLE ROWBARROW
(Bronze Age round barrows)

Location and parking SS 875 415. The barrows are situated on National Trust land, and are reached from the Cloutsham to Hillhead Cross road. There is a small car park on the east of the road at SS 871 418, marked by a National Trust stone pillar with 'Dunkery' on it. From here take the worn trackway uphill (south-eastwards). On top of the hill a large cairn (Great Rowbarrow) is on the left of the path. Another cairn is 100 metres to the south-west (right) and is approached by a narrow path through the moorland. Close by is a low heather-covered mound surrounded by a pronounced bank, which is the remains of a saucer barrow. 400 metres to the south-west another round barrow has been recorded but cannot be seen amidst the uneven boggy ground. Rejoin the path at Great Rowbarrow and take the worn trackway eastwards. 350 metres on the left (north) is

Glastonbury Tor, St. Michael's church tower.

Little Rowbarrow, a grass and heather-covered mound with a pile of stones on top.

The barrows can also be approached from Dunkery Beacon, 1.25 kilometres to the east, along a well-worn path.

Access for disabled visitors. None.

Site description. Four round barrows occupy the peak of this ridge, with a fifth downhill on the west. Great Rowbarrow is a cairn composed of large stones, as is the barrow to the south-west, which may have been known as White Barrow, while Little Rowbarrow is a smaller cairn. The one next to White Barrow appears to be a saucer barrow. At least one of the cairns was dug into by R. Fenton in 1807. The barrows are on a parish boundary, and were obviously used as boundary markers.

Reading. Grinsell 1969, 16, 29; Grinsell 1970, 63.

Nearby sites. 1 Alderman's Barrow; 49 Dunkery Beacon; 81 Joaney How and Robin How; 131 Sweetworthy.

71 GREEN BARROW and BRIGHTWORTHY BARROWS

(Bronze Age round barrows)

Location SS 818 345. Five kilometres south-west of Exford. The barrows are situated on Withypool Common, reached by the road leading south-westwards from Withypool. Green Barrow can be seen from the road, and on the skyline the concrete column of the trigonometrical point (428 metres OD) marks the position of the Brightworthy Barrows. There is no right of way across the moorland to these barrows.

Parking. There is roadside parking just east of Green Barrow, on the south side of the road, by the field boundary.

Access for disabled visitors. Green Barrow can be seen from the roadside as well as the concrete column marking the Brightworthy Barrows. Roadside parking by Green Barrow is possible.

Site description. Green Barrow is a heather-covered round barrow fairly close to the road, and formerly on the Hawkridge boundary. It has a pronounced hollow in the centre indicating that it has been dug into in the past. Nearby, but on the crest of the hill, a group of three barrows known

as the Brightworthy Barrows are situated at SS 818 350. However, one barrow was destroyed in 1913 for road metal, and another has been largely removed but is still recognisable as a disc barrow with a circular bank but no mound. The largest barrow is 100 metres to the east and is surrounded by a ditch. The mound is two metres high and is surmounted by a trigonometrical point which is visible from the road.

Reading. Grinsell 1969, 42.

Nearby sites. 41 Cow Castle; 132 Tarr Steps; 141 Wambarrows; 156 Withypool.

Ham Hill, see also **Witcombe**.

72 HAM HILL (Iron Age hillfort)

Location and parking ST 478 172. Six kilometres west of Yeovil. At Stoke-sub-Hamdon take the turning southwards signposted to Ham Hill. The western part of Ham Hill is a country park and there are several car parks in the hillfort interior. The most convenient one is a turning on the left to the Prince of Wales pub (at ST 478 168). Alternatively there is a parking area on the right-hand (west) of the road at ST 478 166.

From the first car park, there is a footpath signposted 'Public Footpath Monument Stoke-S-Hamdon'. This path goes northwards and follows the ramparts of the northern spur of the hillfort, with a steep drop to the west. At the northern end there is open ground with a war memorial. The very uneven ground is the result of former quarrying, and there is a view of present-day quarrying of Ham stone.

The footpath continues eastwards along the top of one of the ramparts. Towards the extreme north-east end, the ramparts are well-defined, with a second rampart discernible at a lower level. Continue southwards along the edge of the ramparts to the Prince of Wales pub.

To see a different part of the hillfort, walk from the first to the second car park, cross the road (leading to Norton), and follow the footpath on the right (west) signposted 'Little Norton, Norton sub Hamdon'. Go to the top of the rampart and follow the footpath southwards, past a car park at ST 478 164. Continue along the path, on the right (west) of which there is a steep drop and on the left old quarries. The ramparts are not always clearly

Ham Hill hillfort, ditch and rampart.

discernible in this part of the hillfort, and often resemble terraces because the ditches have become filled in. Keep to the worn path which goes round the southern part of the hillfort ramparts and joins another path at a T-junction. Go left (uphill) to the stile. To the east, in the valley, the earthworks of Witcombe deserted Medieval village are visible.

From this point there is no further right of way around the ramparts. Cross the stile, turn right and follow the hedge line to the gate by the road. At the cattle grid, turn left and follow the road to the car park.

A further part of the hillfort can be seen by taking the road eastwards to Montacute. Cross the cattle grid and 500 metres further on at ST 488 164 there is room for one vehicle to park near a field gate. At this point the road cuts through the ramparts (possibly at an original entrance); on the south side the rampart can be seen and on the north side a tree-lined hollow way leads northwards from the field gate, probably the hillfort ditch with a rampart on one side.

Access for disabled visitors. There is parking

Iron Age 'Glastonbury style' pot from Ham Hill.

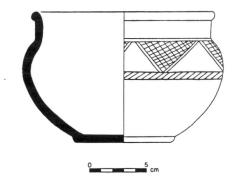

within the interior of the hillfort. The ramparts can also be seen at ST 488 164, and adjacent parking is possible.

Facilities. This is the only hillfort in the country to have a pub in its interior. At the entrance to the car park near the pub, take the first right turning where there are toilets. Nearby is a car park and picnic area.

Site description. Ham or Hamdon Hill is an unusual outcrop of shelly limestone (named Ham stone) occupied by a huge L-shaped hillfort covering 85 hectares. It is the largest such hillfort in Britain: the southern part is a rectangle approx 800 metres x one kilometre, with a northern spur 600 metres x 400 metres, forming an irregular L-shape. In some parts the defences consist of two banks and ditches, while elsewhere the natural escarpment was strengthened by a single ditch and bank. The original entrances have not yet been precisely identified. The site appears to have been utilised in the Neolithic period and Bronze Age, and from the evidence of the pottery there was Iron Age occupation from at least the 7th century BC to the Roman period. The hillfort defences may have been constructed in the later Iron Age (possibly in the 4th or 3rd century BC).

The site was also important during the Roman period as many finds of that date have been discovered as well as a building, possibly a villa. There have been a few Saxon finds but not enough evidence to suggest that the site was refortified in the Saxon period as occurred at nearby South Cadbury. The area around the Prince of Wales pub may have been the hamlet of South Ameldon, the site of an annual fair documented from 1102 to the 17th century, and of local courts. Much of the northern and western parts of the site have been quarried since the Medieval period.

Reading. Burrow 1981, 198-202, 268-77, pls. 9, 10; Morris 1987 (prehistoric pottery); Needham et al (Bronze Age stone moulds).

Nearby sites. 25 Cart Gate; 97 Montacute; 128 Stoke-sub-Hamdon; 153 Witcombe.

Hinkley Point, see **Wick Barrow**.

73 HORNER (Medieval bridge)

Location and parking SS 897 455.
1.25 kilometres south-east of Porlock. There is a car park on the north side of the village. From here walk back to the road and turn left (south). After 30 metres, opposite the garden of the first house, there is an unsignposted trackway known as Hacketty Way on the right (west) of the road leading into Horner Wood (National Trust, open to the public). After a few metres the stream (Horner

Horner, packhorse bridge.

Water) is crossed by the bridge.

Access for disabled visitors. Access can be difficult along the narrow track. There are toilets in the car park.

Facilities. There are toilets and a picnic area in the car park, and refreshments in the village.

Site description. The bridge is a single-arched packhorse bridge, probably of Medieval date. It has a cobbled surface and a steep humped back.

Reading. Jervoise 1930, 113-14.

Nearby sites. 23 Bury Castle; 28 Chapel Cross; 120 Selworthy; 148 West Luccombe.

74 HORSINGTON (Medieval village cross)

Location ST 702 238. Five kilometres SSW of Wincanton. Turn off the A357 road eastwards to Horsington, and after 300 metres take the lane on the right-hand side to the church. The cross is on the left-hand side, on a small green opposite the entrance to Horsington House Hotel.

Parking. In the lane leading to the church.

Access for disabled visitors. It is possible to park right by the cross.

Huish Champflower Bronze Age round barrow.

Site description. The cross appears to be in its original position - now a small green, and probably marks the site of the village market. It consists of four circular hamstone steps with a square socket. The tapering octagonal shaft is quite worn and has a rare sculptured scene on the south side, including a full-length figure (possibly a friar). Below there is an animal's head, and above two skulls (or death's heads) are featured. The cross dates to the 13th century, and may have been a preaching cross, with the sculptured figures being intended to deter wrongdoers. It is also thought that the cross may have been erected in 1284 to mark the grant of free warren by Edward I to William Russell, which included the right to hold a fair, market and a court. The head of the cross is missing: in about 1708 a sun-dial was erected on the top secured by an iron rod which gave way in the mid 19th century; the sun-dial and part of the shaft fell to the ground. Information about the cross is on a nearby stone.

Reading. Pooley 1877, 108-10.

Nearby sites. 6 Balland's Castle; 89 Maperton; 123 South Cadbury Castle; 129 Stowell.

75 HUISH CHAMPFLOWER BARROW (Bronze Age barrow)

Location ST 028 341. Eight kilometres northwest of Wiveliscombe. Turn left (south) off the B3190 road at Brendon Hill, one kilometre west of Ralegh's Cross. Further along this road is a bungalow on the left, before which is a field gate on the right (west) from where the barrow can be seen. A public footpath traverses the field from this gate.

Parking. There is roadside parking.

Access for disabled visitors. The barrow is visible from the field gate by the road.

Site description. This Bronze Age round barrow was planted with larches in about 1830, and was encircled by a wall and bank on which beech trees were planted. Trees are now growing over the entire barrow. The barrow is 21 metres in diameter and was partly excavated in 1903 by Sir Walter Trevelyan, owner of the land, and the Rev. Preb. F. Hancock. The excavations were inconclusive and Gray thought that it might be a Roman barrow.

Reading. Gray 1903; Grinsell 1969, 34.

Nearby sites. 37 Clatworthy Camp; 114, 115 Ralegh's Cross; 157 Wiveliscombe Barrow.

76 HUNTER'S LODGE INN
(Bronze Age barrow or henge)

Location ST 559 498. Four kilometres north of Wells. The site is on the south side of the Wells Road (from Priddy to the A39 road), one kilometre east of the Hunter's Lodge Inn crossroads. It is visible from the road in a pasture field close to a modern block-built barn with a corrugated roof.

Parking. There is a large layby (also used as a store for stone chippings) 400 metres to the east, also on the south side of the road.

Access for disabled visitors. The site is visible from the road but adjacent parking is difficult.

Site description. The site appears as a large dip or hollow, in the centre of which is a mound. It is just over 46 metres in overall diameter, and is possibly a Bronze Age disc barrow or less likely a henge monument. It consists of a low mound surrounded by a ditch and an outer bank. The interior mound is about 18 metres in diameter and 0.3 metres high.

Reading. Allcroft 1908, 528; Grinsell 1971, 113, 126.

Nearby sites. 3 Ashen Hill Barrows; 77, 78 Hunter's Lodge Inn; 112 Priddy Nine Barrows.

77 HUNTER'S LODGE INN
(Bronze Age round barrow)

Location ST 550 501. Four kilometres north of Wells, in a pasture field to the south of the Wells Road (from Priddy to A39 road), just east of the Hunter's Lodge Inn crossroads.

Parking. Roadside parking is difficult as the road is busy.

Access for disabled visitors. Because the road is busy, it can be difficult to park to see the barrow.

Site description. A round barrow, probably Bronze Age in date, is visible as a small mound. It was excavated in about 1924.

Reading. Grinsell 1971, 113.

Nearby sites. 3 Ashen Hill Barrows; 76, 78 Hunter's Lodge Inn; 112 Priddy Nine Barrows.

78 HUNTER'S LODGE INN
(Bronze Age round barrow)

Location ST 559 501. Four kilometres north of Wells. On the north side of the Wells Road (from Priddy to A39 road), one kilometre east of the Hunter's Lodge Inn crossroads. The barrow is visible from the road in a pasture field to the west of a large modern barn, near a track (signposted 'Mountain Ash').

Parking. There is limited roadside parking near the track. Alternatively, park 400 metres east on the south of the road in a large layby used as a store for stone chippings.

Access for disabled visitors. The site is visible from the road, with limited roadside parking.

Site description. This Bronze Age round barrow is a bell barrow with a berm, ditch and outer bank. It is about 40 metres in diameter and one metre high, but has been badly damaged by numerous trial lead mine shafts which also occur elsewhere in the field.

Reading. Grinsell 1971, 113, 126.

Nearby sites. 3 Ashen Hill Barrows; 76, 77 Hunter's Lodge Inn; 112 Priddy Nine Barrows.

79 ILCHESTER (Roman and Medieval town)

Location and parking ST 522 228. Ilchester was once at the junction of two Roman roads, now the A303 and A37 (Fosse Way to Exeter, and the road to Dorchester), but now the A303 by-passes the town and the surrounding road pattern has been drastically altered. The High Street and West Street are no longer a through-route, and roadside parking is usually available. There is also a car park in Limington Road.

Facilities. There are a few shops, garages and eating places, and toilets are opposite the car park in Limington Road.

Access for disabled visitors. There are no problems in visiting the town itself. Toilets are situated opposite the car park in Limington Road.

Site description. Ilchester may have started as an Iron Age oppidum ('town'): a bank and ditch enclosure has been detected to the south of the town on aerial photographs. Ilchester itself was on slightly raised ground above the flood plain of the River Yeo. A Roman military fort, probably a conquest fort, was built at the crossing of the River Yeo along the Fosse Way, and a second fort may also have existed. A town grew up around the fort from the 1st century, originally with timber buildings. When the military forces withdrew,

the civilian site developed, and Ilchester became an important regional town, probably called
Lendiniae (sometimes abbreviated to Lindinis).
Around AD 200, earthwork defences were constructed at the centre of the settlement enclosing
at least ten hectares, and at the end of the 3rd
century these were strengthened by the addition
of a massive stone wall. The timber-framed buildings were also gradually replaced in stone, and
occupation extended beyond the walls, although
the development of the town must have always
been curtailed by the low-lying ground.

Little is known about the street layout and
buildings of the Roman town, but it was strategi-
cally sited for communication and must have been
an important market centre. There were cemeteries
outside the town, mainly along the Fosse Way,
with a large cemetery at Northover by the river,
where lead and stone coffins have been found. The
town declined by the 5th century, and may have
become virtually deserted, but it revived in the late
Saxon and early Medieval period. The Roman
town walls were refurbished in the 10th century, and subsequently new walls were built in
front of these defences, with four town gates. A
Dominican Friary was established in the town
before 1261, part of which was still visible at the
end of the 18th century, and there were at least six
parish churches inside the town walls. For much of
the period up to 1846 Ilchester was the county
town of Somerset. However, by the late 14th
century, the town had declined and the population
was much reduced.

Several excavations have taken place in the
town, and a few finds are on display in the
museum at Ilchester, while others are in the
County Museum, Taunton. It is regrettable that
virtually nothing is visible of this once important
Roman town, and that very little of the Medieval
town can also be seen, apart from the church of St.
Mary Major which is the only Medieval church in
Ilchester to have survived.

Reading. Aston & Leech 1977, 67-72, pl.6,
maps 27-29; Burnham & Wacher 1990, 62-70;
Dunning 1974a, 179-83; Leach & Dunning 1990;
Leech & Leach 1982, 76-80.

Nearby sites. 80 Ilchester; 96, 97 Montacute;
147 West Camel.

80 ILCHESTER (Museum)

Location ST 521 227. The museum is situated in
the High Street (opposite no. 2 High Street), round
the corner from the old Town Hall, and near the
Dolphin pub.

Parking. There is roadside parking near the
museum.

Access for disabled visitors. None.

Facilities. There is a small sales area, and refreshments are available in the town. Toilets are opposite the Limington Road car park.

Admission charge. A charge is made.

Open. Thursdays and Saturdays, Easter to the
end of September, 10am-4pm.

The Museum. Comprises one room, with displays of Roman finds from the town of Ilchester,
including a lead coffin and skeleton, as well as finds
of later date and a few local history objects.

Nearby sites. 79 Ilchester; 96, 97 Montacute;
147 West Camel.

81 JOANEY HOW and ROBIN HOW
(Bronze Age round barrows)

Location and parking SS 907 427.
4.25 kilometres SSE of Porlock. There is a car park
on the east side of the road from Chapel Cross to
Dunkery Gate at SS 904 422. Walk along the road
northwards for about 100 metres to SS 905 425,
where there is a worn trackway (at a point known
as Rex Stile Head) leading north-eastwards to the
barrows across the stoney heather moorland. The
path approaches the largest cairn, on the top of the
hill, which is known as the Beacon. 75 metres to its
north-west is another large cairn, known as Robin
How, and 75 metres to the north-east is the cairn
known as Joaney How, surrounded by a ditch. Further down the hillside there are at least eight other
smaller cairns, some covered by moorland vegetation.

Access for disabled visitors. Robin How and
the Beacon are visible on the skyline from the
road, but otherwise there is no access.

Site description. This is a group of Bronze Age
round barrows, all of which are cairns built of large
stones, some of which have been piled up with
additional stones in recent years. They are situated
on the north-eastern part of the Dunkery Hill ridge
and on the slopes of the hill, mainly the north-east,

on National Trust land. The three largest cairns are known as Joaney How, Robin How (in the centre) and the Beacon. The parish boundary runs across the ridge through the barrows, which are likely to have been used as boundary markers.

The Beacon has been used as a fire beacon in the past, and Joaney How and Robin How may have been used for the same purpose. The origin of the names of the latter two cairns is uncertain. Until the mid 19th century they were known as the Luccombe barrows, and the names of Joaney How and Robin How first appear on an Ordnance Survey map of 1889. The name 'How' may derive from Old Norse, and 'Howe' is commonly used for barrows in northern England. Alternatively, they may reflect an ancient legend surrounding Robin Hood and Little John. Without evidence for the names being used earlier than 1889, their derivation must be treated with caution.

Reading. Grinsell 1969, 14, 15, 17, 43; Grinsell 1970, 58, 63, 116, 154.

Nearby sites. 28 Chapel Cross; 49 Dunkery Beacon; 73 Horner; 131 Sweetworthy.

82 KENWALCH'S CASTLE (Castle Wood), Penselwood (Iron Age hillfort)

Location ST 747 335. 6.6 kilometres ESE of Bruton. Take the road northwards from Penselwood, and the hillfort is two kilometres distant. The road (also the county boundary) cuts through the middle of the hillfort, and there is very dense woodland on the east (Wiltshire) side and less dense woodland on the west (Somerset) side. On the north side of the hillfort, the rampart can be seen where it is cut by the road. On the south side a trackway passes through the wood on either side of the road (where there is also a sign about horseriding), and a stretch of the fairly substantial ramparts can be seen here.

Parking. There is roadside parking at the southern end of the hillfort.

Access for disabled visitors. The hillfort can be viewed from the road.

Site description. Kenwalch's Castle or Castle Wood is situated within an area of woodland which completely covers its defences and interior. It consists of an area of 1.6 hectares, and has a single rampart and ditch, well preserved in places,

up to 5.5 metres above the ditch. The road probably passes through the original entrances.

Reading. Burrow 1924, 112, 113 (figure); Burrow 1981, 238-9.

Nearby sites. 6 Balland's Castle; 20 Bruton; 126 Stavordale Priory; 155 Witham Friary.

83 KILVE (Medieval chantry ruins)

Location ST 146 440. 5.5 kilometres north-west of Nether Stowey. At Kilve turn northwards into Sea Lane off the A39 road by the Post Office and the pub. Continue for just over one kilometre, past the church, and the chantry ruins are on the left adjacent to Chantry Cottage. The ruins are marked by 'Danger. Keep Out' signs.

Parking. The large Kilve Pylle car park is just north of the chantry ruins on the left (west) of the road.

Access for disabled visitors. The ruins are visible from the road, and there is adjacent parking. Toilets are at the north end of the car park.

Facilities. Refreshments are available in this part of Kilve, and the car park is also a picnic site. Toilets are at the north end of the car park – to reach them, turn left by the brick building (an old oil retort) and go over a little bridge.

Site description. In 1329 Sir Simon de Furneaux gave an endowment of lands to maintain a chantry to pray for his soul and those of his wife and ancestors. The manor house was given as the residence for the college of priests, and the chantry chapel was on the north side of the nearby church. It appears that the college was short-lived and that Kilve Chantry was dissolved by the end of the 14th century. The manor house was then used as a farmhouse and came to be known as the Priory or Kilve Priory. It was a substantial 13th century Medieval house with a hall range on the west, and on the east there was a cross wing with a solar and a chapel on the first floor. From the mid 17th century, it was known as Kilve Farm. Part of the building was used for storage, possibly mainly by smugglers who used this part of the coast a great deal, and in 1848 the eastern part of the manor house was destroyed in a fire. At the time, inflammable casks of spirits are suspected to have been stored in the building. In 1977 the western part of the manor house was divided into Priory and

Kilve, chantry ruins.

Chantry Cottages, while the eastern part with the chapel remains as a picturesque but decaying ivy-covered ruin.

Reading. Dunning 1985a, 99; Waite 1969, 67-9.

Nearby sites. 47 Dowsborough; 85 Lilstock; 127 Stogursey; 137 Trendle Ring.

King John's Hunting Lodge , see **Axbridge.**

84 KINGSDOWN CAMP (Iron Age hillfort)

Location and parking ST 719 517. 4.5 kilometres south-east of Radstock. From the A362 (Radstock-Frome) road, take the road westwards at ST 724 519. After 500 metres, just past the sawmills, is a verge on the left (south) side by a trackway (Green Lane). The bank of the hillfort is visible in the adjacent pasture field, and traces of a ditch can be seen. An unmarked footpath leads along Green Lane and turns south-west into the field alongside the field boundary.

Access for disabled visitors. The hillfort is partly visible from the roadside.

Site description. This small hillfort encloses 0.15 hectares, and is partly hidden within Kingsdown Wood. Excavations have shown that it was a univallate Iron Age hillfort with a bank and ditch. Either in the Iron Age or in the Roman period, a drystone wall was constructed, possibly four metres high and 2.5 metres wide, and the site then continued to be occupied in the Roman period. The bank of the hillfort can be seen in the field, but the ditch is barely visible. The hillfort is approximately quadrilateral in shape and had an entrance on the north-east side.

Reading. Burrow 1981, 144-5, 260, 301-2.

Nearby sites. 14 Blacker's Hill; 63 Frome; 90 Marston; 103 Nunney.

Kit Barrows, see **Dunkery Beacon.**

85 LILSTOCK, St. Andrew's Church
(Medieval church ruin)

Location ST 167 448. 5.5 kilometres north-west of Nether Stowey. On the right-angle bend on the A39 road at ST 159 422, take the turning northwards signposted to Kilton and Lilstock. Continue along the road for nearly three kilometres. Fifty metres before the road bears right to Lilstock, there is a short grassed trackway on the right (east) side of the road, at the end of which is a gate leading to the churchyard.

Parking. Parking is possible in the trackway.

Access for disabled visitors. The site is extremely overgrown and can only be viewed from the gate.

Site description. A church existed at Lilstock from at least the early 12th century, and in 1251 it was appropriated by Stogursey priory. It passed to Eton College around 1442 on the dissolution of the priory, and by 1532 it was known as St. Andrew's Church. In 1554 the chancel needed repair and the windows were said to be in a ruinous state. In 1791 the church was reported to be a small building 18.25 metres long and 4.25 metres wide. A painting of 1845 shows the church with a chancel, nave with south porch, and an embattled west tower, apparently of 14th century date. In 1881, on the annexation of the parish to Kilton, the church was demolished except for the chancel which was remodelled as a mortuary chapel, with the addition of a porch and bell-cote. This chapel was declared redundant in 1980, and the 12th century font was removed to Stogursey church in 1981. Traces of the entire Medieval church are visible as a depression in the churchyard when it is not overgrown, but at the moment it is neglected and the chapel is in need of repair.

To the south of the church there are indications of a more extensive settlement, with house platforms being recorded in a nearby field. A parsonage house formerly existed at Lilstock as well; in 1557 it was in need of repair and by 1827 only part of a wall was standing.

Reading. Dunning 1985b, 103, 106-7.

Nearby sites. 83 Kilve; 101 Nether Stowey; 127 Stogursey; 152 Wick Barrow.

Little Rowbarrow, see **Great Rowbarrow and Little Rowbarrow**.

86 LORD'S LOT (Bronze Age round barrow)

Location ST 522 552. Six kilometres ENE of Cheddar. Situated near Nordrach on the south-west side of the B3134 road, 300 metres north-west of the crossroads (junction of B3134 and B3371 roads).

Parking. There is very limited parking near a gateway on the opposite side of the road.

Access for disabled visitors. Visible from the road.

Site description. This prominent Bronze Age round barrow is close to the road and is one of many examples in this area of the Mendips.

Reading. Grinsell 1971, 102

Nearby sites. 30, 32 ,33, Charterhouse-on-Mendip; 159 Wright's Piece.

Luccombe, see **Chapel Cross**.

87 MADACOMBE (Bronze Age round barrows)

Location and parking SS 828 426. 6.5 kilometres south-west of Porlock. The barrows are reached from the road from Lucott Cross to Wellshead. There is roadside parking just past Alderman's Barrow and before the cattle grid (at SS 835 422), near the National Trust sign for Dunkery. On the west of the road is a stile and gate, signposted to 'Doone Valley 3½, Malmshead 6' and by the stile is an Exmoor National Park information board about the Larkbarrow estate. Walk along the wide track north-westwards for 750 metres. On the right is a mound, beyond which is another such mound.

Access for disabled visitors. None

Site description. These two Bronze Age heather-covered round barrows are situated close to a stone row of ten stones which is concealed by the vegetation.

Reading. Grinsell 1969, 32.

Nearby sites. 1 Alderman's Barrow; 43 Culbone Hill; 107 Porlock Common; 151 Whit Stones.

88 MAESBURY CASTLE (Iron Age hillfort)

Location ST 610 471. Three kilometres NNW of Shepton Mallet. The shortest route is from a footpath off the north side of the Old Frome Road at ST 607 471, 300 metres south-east of the disused railway. The footpath is signposted: go over the stile by the metal gate, and cross the field diagonally (eastwards) up the steep slope to the woods. At the corner of the field is a metal gate and a stile. Go over the stile, and the hillfort is right in front. The footpath goes north-eastwards over the ditch, up the steep rampart, across the interior of the hillfort, and over the rampart and down into the ditch on the other side.

Parking. There is very limited roadside parking along the Old Frome Road; a better road in which to park runs southwards to Croscombe off the Old Frome Road, nearly opposite the footpath.

Access for disabled visitors. None, and the hillfort is not visible from the roadside.

Site description. This Iron Age hillfort of Maesbury (or Masbury) Castle (or Camp) is a roughly oval enclosure covering 2.8 hectares at 290 metres OD. The defences consist primarily of a rampart, still standing six metres high above an outer ditch, with entrances on the north-west and south-east. In the past the entrance on the north-west has been observed to have traces of additional earthworks, possibly forming an outwork defending the entrance. The south-east entrance has been considerably widened and the ditch filled in. On the northern side of the hillfort there is evidence for an additional bank and ditch. In AD 705 the site was known as 'Merksburi' ('fort on the boundary'), and in the 15th century William Worcestre wrote 'Maesbury Castle was built on a high hill by a giant called Merk. It was thrown down, but more than a hundred thousand cartloads of stone are heaped there.'

Reading. Burrow 1924, 80, 81 (figure); Burrow 1981, 223-4, pl.1; Gray 1908; Tratman 1959.

Nearby sites. 10 Beacon Hill; 14 Blacker's Hill; 149, 150 Whitnell Corner.

89 MAPERTON (Saxon sculptured stone)

Location   ST 672 261. 4.25 kilometres south-west of Wincanton. The sculptured stone is set in the west wall of the south porch of the parish church of SS. Peter & Paul. The church is approached by a narrow secluded trackway bounded by a high wall and a line of beech trees, to the east of Maperton House.

Parking. Small vehicles can go up the trackway

Maperton Saxon sculptured stone.

where there is parking space by the church. Otherwise there is roadside parking 100 metres to the west at the wide intersection of the two roads in the centre of the village.

Access for disabled visitors. There is level access, and parking outside the church for small vehicles.

Site description. The sculptured stone was recovered during the rebuilding of the church in the 19th century. It is a sub-rectangular slab with a foliate design. It is 0.55 metres high and 0.39 metres wide, and may date to the 10th century.

Reading. Foster 1987, 56, 58, 76, fig. 7d.

Nearby sites. 26 Castle Cary; 74 Horsington; 123 South Cadbury Castle; 129 Stowell.

90 MARSTON (Deserted Medieval Village)

Location and parking ST 769 448.
2.5 kilometres south of Frome. Follow the A361 road from Nunney to Frome, and turn right at the roundabout (numbered A361). Turn right almost immediately (signposted to Tytherington). At Tytherington there is parking space by a tele-

Marston Magna, ridge-and-furrow.

phone, post box and large driveway nearly opposite the pub. From here (ST 768 452) an unsignposted footpath leads to Lower Marston, passing very close to the deserted village.

The deserted village is also visible in a pasture field 150 metres south of Tytherington on the west (right) of the road. Roadside parking is possible. Then turn right (signposted Trudoxhill) where the deserted village is visible from the first field gate on the north of the road, and in a small area of the field to the south of the road.

Access for disabled visitors. Parts of the site can be viewed from the roadside (see above).

Site description. The earthworks are all that is visible of the deserted Medieval village. Earthworks of a hollow way (the former village street), and of garden plots lining the street, survive up to a height of 1.2 metres. A village was mentioned at Marston in 1155, but it was probably destroyed during the 18th century emparking by the owners of Marston House.

Nearby sites. 63 Frome; 92 Marston Moat; 103 Nunney Castle; 154 Witham.

91 MARSTON MAGNA (Medieval moated site and ridge-and-furrow)

Location and parking ST 594 222. Six kilometres north-east of Yeovil. There is a car park behind the village hall on the west of the A359

road at ST 591 223, or limited parking closer to the site by St. Mary's Church and the Post Office. The site is immediately south-west of the church. Walk along Garston Lane to the south of the church and go over the stile by the field gate. The footpath is signposted to Rimpton, and crosses the pasture field diagonally. Many earthworks are visible in the field. At the next field boundary there is a stile, and the footpath goes across ridge-and-furrow in this next field.

Access for disabled visitors. The earthworks are visible from the field gate, or from the churchyard (access at the west end of the churchyard is by two shallow steps).

Site description. Marston Magna Medieval moated site is owned by Somerset County Council. Extending over almost the entire field (known as Court Garden) there is a large rectangular moat and other earthworks including two possible fishponds and house platforms. The moat is trapezoidal in shape and would once have had a bridge; the flat-bottomed ditch is up to 17.6 metres in width and 2.2 metres deep. The moat platform would have contained buildings. The site is unusual in still being associated with an excellent example of broad ridge-and-furrow (in the field known as Garston Field), as most examples of Medieval field systems associated with moated sites have been ploughed flat.

The site is Medieval in date, but the precise dating is uncertain. It has been recently surveyed

The abbot's manor house at Meare.

by the Royal Commission on the Historical Monuments of England (Exeter).

Reading. Aston & Dennison 1988, 399, fig. 5; Brown et al 1988, 117, fig. 7.7.

Nearby sites. 79 Ilchester; 100 Nether Adber; 123 South Cadbury Castle; 147 West Camel.

92 MARSTON MOAT (Medieval moated site)

Location. ST 767 438. 3.5 kilometres SSW of Frome. Going south from Tytherington, turn right (signposted Trudoxhill), past Moat Farm on the left and Thickthorn Cottage on the right. Turn left (south) up a no-through road, and the moated site is on the left, visible from the road.

Parking. There is very limited roadside parking.

Access for disabled visitors. The site can be viewed from the roadside.

Site description. The rectangular moated area was the site of the mansion of the Bigot family and the manor house of Marston. It was built before 1195, and was fortified without licence by Richard Bigot, which displeased Edward II. By the reign of Edward IV it seems to have been let as a farmhouse. The site was probably damp and unhealthy, being in a low-lying position on wet clay near the River Frome. It is not known when it became deserted, but a later mansion (Marston House) was built only one kilometre away, possibly in the early 17th century.

Marston Moat is now overgrown with woodland, although the substantial outer bank is visible from the road. The moat is six metres wide and surrounds an island 37 metres x 33 metres. In Bowen's map of Somerset, published in 1760, it is labelled 'Roman Mount', but Sir Richard Colt Hoare visited the site on 27 March 1808 and remarked 'It is only the relict of a moated mansion house'.

Reading. McGarvie 1974, 15-16.

Nearby sites. 90 Marston; 103 Nunney Castle; 154 Witham; 155 Witham Friary.

Martock, see **Cart Gate**.

93 MEARE FISH HOUSE (Medieval monastic building)

Location and parking ST 458 417. Five kilometres north-west of Glastonbury. The site is signposted off the Glastonbury Road, 250 metres east of the parish church. There is very restricted parking in the narrow no-through lane leading northwards off the B3151 Glastonbury Road, adjacent to the pasture field in which the fish house is situated. The site is in the care of English Heritage. To view the interior, the key may be obtained from Manor House Farm (Meare Farm) situated at ST 455 417 at the rear of the church. The farm is not signposted but may be reached by taking the footpath past the fish house across the field, or by going along the road.

Meare Fish House.

Access for disabled visitors. There is no level access into the field, but the fish house is visible from the gateway.

Open. At any reasonable time.

Site description. The fish house was the home of the chief fisherman to Glastonbury Abbey and was probably used to salt and store fish caught in Meare Pool. It now stands in the middle of a field, but was once very close to Meare Pool, a huge shallow lake and an important fishery. In 1537 Leland described the pool 'at high Waters in Winter a 4 Miles in Cumpace', but by 1741 it was no longer a permanent body of water. The fish house is surrounded by earthworks which seem to represent three fishponds, possibly used to store fish that had been caught. The building had two storeys with workshops below and lodgings above and an outside staircase. It dates to the early 14th century.

Meare Farm to the west was once the ab-bot's manor house, contemporary with the fish house. Despite it being altered in the 17th century, many original features survive including the blocked arches of the three great windows of a first-floor hall on the south facade (to the east of the porch). The tower and chancel of the nearby parish church are also early 14th century in date, but the nave and aisles are later.

Reading. Aston & Dennison 1988, 394-5, figs. 3, 4.

Nearby sites. 67, 68 Glastonbury; 94 Meare; 104 Peat Moors Visitors Centre.

94 MEARE, Lake Villages
(Iron Age settlement sites)

Location and parking ST 446 421.

5.2 kilometres SSE of Wedmore. The site is in pasture fields just south of the River Brue, but virtually nothing is visible. At Westhay take the minor road eastwards (to Oxenpill) by Westhay Cottage and the Bird in Hand pub. On the south side of the road there are two cottages (Long Cottage and North View) between which is a field gate on the north side of the road. From here there is a general view northwards across the site, and low mounds can sometimes be discerned depending on the state of vegetation.

Access for disabled visitors. The site can be viewed from the field gate.

Site description. Two adjacent Iron Age villages of exceptional importance (Meare East and Meare West) were discovered in 1895 by Arthur Bulleid. Excavations took place intermittently on both sites by Arthur Bulleid and Harold St. George Gray from 1910 to 1956. Excavations also took place in 1966 and 1968-9 and again more recently. The Medieval Meare Pool came to cover the site, once a huge tract of water up to four miles in circumference, but by the mid 18th century it was no longer a permanent body of water.

Although close to Glastonbury Lake Village, the Meare sites were rather different and were never actually a 'lake village'. They consisted of two groups of mounds each constructed on the edge of a small patch of raised bog, with a dry island to the south and a lake to the north-east. The two settlements were separated by a narrow area of swamp and by water. At both sites clay was deliberately dumped and renewed from time to time, and eventually mounds were formed from the accumulation of clay and occupation debris. Little evidence for buildings has been found, although at Meare Village West there was evidence for extensive timberwork, with hundreds of wooden timbers and stakes, some of which may have been huts and fences. Very little timberwork has been found at Meare Village East, and occupation there may have been in tents on a seasonal basis. Nearly two hundred hearths have been found, mainly at Meare Village East.

Because Meare was never as wet as Glastonbury, a similar range of organic objects did not survive. Many other types of Iron Age finds have been excavated, though, including amber beads, bone needles and toggles, baked clay loom-weights, antler combs, fine quality pottery (some decorated) and coloured glass beads. Bone and antler were worked on the site, as well as glass and possibly bronze and other metals.

Meare Village West was occupied from the 3rd century BC, while the nearby site of Meare Village East was occupied fifty to one hundred years later from the 2nd century BC, possibly on a seasonal basis. Occupation may have continued until the

1st or 2nd century AD in the Roman period, when the sites were probably abandoned due to severe flooding. Although once a waterlogged site, the drainage of the area in recent times has resulted in a significant lowering of the water table, so that the organic remains such as wood are gradually drying out and therefore being destroyed without ever being excavated, and burrowing animals are now damaging the site as well.

Reading. Coles 1987; Coles 1989, 140-4.

Nearby sites. 68 Glastonbury, Lake Village; 93 Meare Fish House; 104 Peat Moors Visitors Centre; 144 Wedmore.

95 MONTACUTE (Medieval cross)

Location ST 496 169. The cross is on the south side of St. Catherine's church by a yew tree in the churchyard.

Parking. There is limited parking near the church, or parking in the village square ('The Borough').

Access for disabled visitors. The main entrance to the churchyard on the north side of the church has two steps, but there is level access on the west side off the no-through road. Parking is possible outside the church.

Facilities. There are refreshments and shops in the village.

Site description. The cross was moved to its present site from the front of the church in the early 19th century. It consists of a socket and a shaft with badly eroded carvings. Pooley identified the carved ecclesiastical figure as being possibly Reginaldus Cancellarius, one of the earliest benefactors to the priory at Montacute in the 12th century.

Reading. Pooley 1877, 49.

Nearby sites. 72 Ham Hill; 96, 97 Montacute; 153 Witcombe.

96 MONTACUTE (Medieval priory)

Location ST 496 168. At the parish church go up the no-through road and along Abbey Farm Private Road (where there are two footpath signs). On the right is Abbey Farm (the priory gatehouse). Turn right across the yard from where the gatehouse can be viewed, although an application

Montacute, the abbey gatehouse.

granted to William Petre in the same year, who leased them to John Urt as a farmhouse (Abbey House), until about 1600. In the meantime Montacute House was built in the 1590s, and the former priory lands and Abbey House became part of the Phelips estate. Abbey Farm, the priory gatehouse, still survives and has been a residence since the 16th century. It is a fine survival of a priory gatehouse. In the field south of the church, earthworks represent the position of former buildings, and one of the monastic fishponds and the priory's dovecote can still be seen.

Reading. Aston & Dennison 1988, 395; Dunning 1974b, 214; Scott Holmes 1911, 111-15.

Nearby sites. 72 Ham Hill; 95, 97 Montacute; 153 Witcombe.

to divert this footpath has been submitted. Go back to the private road, turn right along the gravelled bridle path. In the field on the left are earthworks and the fishpond of the priory, with the square dovecote on the far side of the field. On the right go past a barn, converted to three dwellings. Then turn right, following the yellow waymark signs across the paddock along the permissive footpath. From here the rear of the priory gatehouse can be viewed.

Parking. There is limited parking near the church, or parking in the village square ('The Borough').

Access for disabled visitors. Parking is sometimes possible near the church, with level access as far as Abbey Farm. The gravelled bridle path prevents further easy access.

Facilities. There are refreshments and shops in the village.

Site description. Towards the end of the 11th century a Cluniac priory was founded by William of Mortain at Montacute. The history of the priory is fairly well documented, and includes debts incurred by the priory in the 12th-13th centuries. In 1279 the prior was accused of clipping coins, and was dismissed for the same offence in 1284. The priory was dissolved in 1539 and the monastic church seems to have been demolished immediately. The surviving buildings and land were

97 MONTACUTE, St. Michael's Hill
(Medieval castle)

Location and parking ST 493 169. The site of the castle is on St. Michael's Hill which, with its 18th century tower, dominates the village of Montacute.

The hill can be reached from footpaths from Montacute Abbey Farm, but the easiest route is to follow the Montacute Road towards Stoke-sub-Hamdon. There is a small car park by the recreation ground on the south side of the road, opposite the telephone kiosk and Mason Lane. Walk across the recreation ground and the next two fields towards the tree-covered St. Michael's Hill, following the footpath signs. Cross the stile and follow the waymark signs to the summit.

Access for disabled visitors. None, but St. Michael's Hill is visible from a distance.

Site description. The hill is owned by the National Trust. A manuscript from Waltham Abbey *De Inventione Sancte Crucis*, written soon after 1177, records the legend of the finding of a miraculous cross on top of the hill in the time of Cnut (around 1035). Tovi (or Tofig), who owned large estates in Somerset and Essex, took it to Waltham, Essex, where a church (later becoming Waltham Abbey) was built to house the cross and where the cross continued to work miracles. The cross came into the hands of King Harold after the

St Michael's Hill and Montacute House, an 18th century engraving.

death of Tovi, and the Holy Cross was used as a war cry by the English against the Normans. A castle was built on top of the hill soon after the Norman conquest in 1066 by Robert, Count of Mortain. The construction of a castle on top of the hill was apparently a final insult to the English, who besieged the castle in 1068.

Together with Dunster, Montacute is one of only two Somerset castles mentioned in the Domesday Book of 1086. St. Michael's Hill is a natural conical hill and it was scarped to form a steep-sided motte which was flattened on top. Below it on the south-east side was a small upper bailey, with a lower bailey on a plateau around the hill. It is difficult to discern these features as the castle mound has been wooded since the late 18th century. The village of Montacute took its name from the hill, the *Mons acutus*. There is some evidence that the castle was built of stone, which would be very unusual for such an early castle. The castle appears to have soon lost its strategic importance and it was given to the newly-founded priory at Montacute around 1102. According to Leland, writing in the mid 16th century, the castle was then partly demolished and the materials used in the priory.

A chapel existed on the castle site by about 1102. It was dedicated to St. Michael and was either originally part of the castle or was built on the castle ruins. It was reached by a flight of stone steps and was itself built of stone. It was still in existence by 1630, but by 1760 it had disappeared and a folly tower was built on the site, which is still standing. Footings can be seen beneath the northern part of the tower which appear to relate to an earlier building, possibly the chapel.

Reading. Adkins & Adkins 1989b; Bascombe 1989, 478; Dunning 1974b, 212, 215; Pooley 1877, 49-58 (with an extensive description of the Legend of the Holy Cross).

Nearby sites. 72 Ham Hill; 95, 96 Montacute; 153 Witcombe.

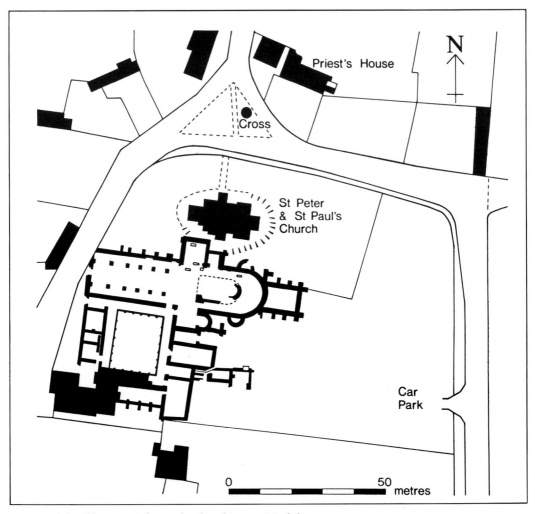

Location of the Abbey, priest's house, church and cross at Muchelney.

98 MUCHELNEY (Saxon and Medieval monastery)

Location ST 428 248. 1.75 kilometres SSE of Langport. Muchelney Abbey ruins are to the south of the parish church, but can only be partly viewed from the churchyard. The abbey is in the care of English Heritage.

Parking. There is a car park (signposted) on the east side of the abbey, just to the south of the village centre and church.

Access for disabled visitors. There is access to much of the site, but not the upper storeys. There are toilets in Cocklemoor car park, Langport.

Facilities. There is a sales area and toilets.

Admission charge. English Heritage charges.

Open. Good Friday or 1 April (whichever is earlier) to 30 September, daily 10am-6pm. Closed for lunch 1-2pm.

Site description. Muchelney (the name means 'large island') lies in the south of the Somerset Levels on an area of ground just high enough to protect it from winter floods. A monastery was founded on the site in the Saxon period. A charter, long thought to be a Medieval forgery, attributed the founding of the monastery to King Ine in 693. The monastery was certainly in existence by 762 when King Cynewulf made a grant to it, and excavation in the 1950's revealed foundations of

Muchelney Abbey, winter flooding.

a Saxon church beneath the Medieval monastic church. As such, it is the second oldest monastery in Somerset, the oldest being at Glastonbury.

The first monastery at Muchelney was possibly destroyed by the Danes in the 870's, but it was refounded in 939 by King Athelstan as part of his penance for executing his brother Edwin. In the 10th century it became a Benedictine monastery dedicated to SS. Peter and Paul. The abbey prospered, and by the 12th century there were twenty-four monks. It owned a great deal of land, although never on the same scale as Glastonbury Abbey.

The local people probably initially used the monastic church, but a separate parish church was built – only one metre from the north transept of the monastic church. In the early 14th century a house was built for the parish priest, which is now known as the 'Priest's House'. It stands to the north of the parish church and is a rare survival of a Medieval vicarage. It was altered in the 15th century, and was purchased by the National Trust in 1911. It can be visited, but only by prior appointment with the tenant.

There is a legend that around 1430, after many years of separation, two lovers met. One was the Abbot of Muchelney and the other Lady Agnes, a nun of Westover (where there was never a nunnery). The nun was smuggled into a hiding place in

St. Dunstan's Tower in the abbey, but when the opportunity arrived for both of them to flee, she was found dead.

The abbey was dissolved on 3 January 1538 when there were only eleven monks. The monastic church was demolished soon after, along with many of the other buildings. Part of the abbey was used as a farm, but the site of the priory was otherwise lost for three centuries. Many of the buildings in Muchelney can be seen to be constructed from stone taken from the priory. In 1927 the site passed to the care of the Ministry of Works (now English Heritage) and extensive excavations took place which revealed the foundations of many buildings.

The visible remains include the foundations of the abbey church and its small apsidal Saxon predecessor, the sacristy, chapter house, warming house, refectory and cloister. The most impressive part of the abbey is the surviving abbot's house (or lodging) which dates to the early 16th century. As a comfortable residence, it was not demolished, but converted to a farmhouse after the Dissolution and has been much altered over the years. The ground floor and upper floor can be visited, and the abbot's house also contains the ticket office, sales area, toilet, and a room with carved stone fragments.

In the farm to the south-east the two-storied

Muchelney Abbey, The Abbot's Lodging.

thatched reredorter (which contained the latrines) still survives, to which there is only access to the upper floor. In the parish church there are various fragments of building material from the abbey, including an unusual circular setting of glazed floor tiles. The parish church is also worth a visit for its 17th century painted ceiling.

Reading. Hugo 1859; Scott Holmes 1911, 103-7; Taylor & Taylor 1965, 451-3.

Nearby sites. 2 Aller; 39 Coat; 48 Drayton; 99 Muchelney.

99 MUCHELNEY (Medieval cross)

Location ST 429 249. The cross is on the edge of the green between the church and the Priest's House.

Parking. Roadside parking near the church.

Access for disabled visitors. Access is possible, with parking very close by.

Site description. The Medieval cross at Muchelney appears to have been drastically restored, if not entirely replaced, in about 1840 by the lord of the manor, Walter Long. It was apparently rebuilt on the same site as the original cross and was an exact copy, although Pevsner states that the base and shaft of the cross are original. The cross consists of three octagonal steps and a socket. Pooley considered that the original cross would have been surmounted by a cross head with figures, but any design for this was lost. He also deplored the constant acts of vandalism to the cross which were

happening in the late 19th century 'It is much to be deplored that this symbol of our faith is not proof against the Vandalism of the age. From time to time the finial has been hurled to the ground and the shaft broken, and the damage has been as frequently repaired'. The cross is now more in danger of damage by vehicles, as it is so close to a narrow stretch of road.

Reading. Pevsner 1958a, 251; Pooley 1877, 181-2.

Nearby sites. 2 Aller; 39 Coat; 48 Drayton; 98 Muchelney.

100 NETHER ADBER (Deserted Medieval village)

Location and parking ST 588 212.
4.5 kilometres north-east of Yeovil. Going southwards on the A359 road (towards Yeovil), pass the Marston Inn, and after 300 metres take the first turning left. This is Thorny Lane, the northern part of which is a narrow tarmac road. After 250 metres it turns right (west) and then immediately left (south). At this point is a small gate leading into the field on the west of Thorny Lane. The earthworks of the deserted village are within a rectangle 250 metres x 400 metres, covering much of this field and the field to the south (the two fields being separated by Thorny Lane as it turns westwards towards Thorny House). From the gate the footpath goes diagonally across the northern field. Return to the road, and after 270 metres the lane turns westwards. Earthworks are visible in the field to the south. Parking can be difficult as the lane is very narrow.

Access for disabled visitors. Some of the earthworks can be viewed from the roadside.

Site description. The well-preserved earthworks represent house sites, enclosures, and hollow ways, surrounded by ridge-and-furrow field systems. It is the site of the village of Nether Adber, although it is sometimes incorrectly referred to as Thorney or Thorny. A settlement by the name of Thorny may have existed nearby. Nether Adber is mentioned in Domesday as 'Ettebere'. Its later history is well documented (see Aston 1977), and in the 14th century is referred to as 'Netherattebere'. The village seems to have been virtually deserted by the mid 16th century. The northern field once con-

Nether Adber deserted Medieval village surrounded by the remains of ridge-and-furrow field systems, as existed until recent years (Cambridge University Collection: copyright reserved).

sisted of a moated manor, fishpond, chapel and other earthworks, but the field was badly disturbed some twenty years ago when many earthworks were flattened and the hollows filled in. The field to the south consists of a hollow way running north-south, representing the village street, as well as rectangular platforms of houses and rectangular enclosures divided by banks and ditches.

The village was once surrounded by extensive ridge-and-furrow field systems, which are now ploughed flat but are visible from old aerial photographs. The site is now owned by Somerset County Council.

Reading. Aston 1977 (including a plan of the village and surrounding field systems); Aston & Dennison 1989, 117.

Nearby sites. 79 Ilchester; 91 Marston Magna; 123 South Cadbury Castle; 147 West Camel.

101 NETHER STOWEY (Medieval castle)
Location and parking ST 186 395.
10.5 kilometres WNW of Bridgwater. The castle is on the south-west side of Nether Stowey, and is bounded by Mill Lane on the west, Butchers Lane on the north, and Castle Hill on the east. There is limited parking at the west end of the very narrow Butchers Lane, with a stile into the field from where the footpath goes uphill over the castle earthworks to a stile on the other side of the field which leads to the Castle Hill road. There is also a car park adjacent to the library in nearby Castle Street, opposite the Castle Stores.

Access for disabled visitors. The castle is visible on its west side in Mill Lane.

Facilities. Banks, shops and refreshments are in the town, and toilets in the library car park.

Site description. Nether Stowey is an early motte castle with two baileys. It was probably

Nether Stowey, outline of the keep walls on top of the castle motte.

constructed in the early 12th century or before by William Fitzodo, and was certainly in existence by the mid 12th century. It subsequently passed into the ownership of the Audley family. On top of the large flattened motte was a rectangular stone keep about eighteen metres by fifteen metres, probably dating to the mid 12th century. The very pronounced wall foundations of the keep (now grassed over) are visible on top of the motte; it is not known when these foundations were excavated. An impressive moat still survives, as well as bailey earthworks around the edge of the field. The castle was abandoned by 1485.

Reading. Aston & Leech 1977, 110-14, pl. 7, maps 45, 46.

Nearby sites. 45 Dead Woman's Ditch; 47 Dowsborough; 62 Fiddington; 127 Stogursey.

102 NORTON FITZWARREN

(Bronze Age enclosure, Iron Age hillfort)

Location and parking ST 196 262. Three kilometres north-west of Taunton. At ST 196 258 opposite the industrial estate, turn northwards off the A361 road into Blackdown View, a residential street. Further up, just past the school and immediately opposite the churchyard, there is a small car park. From here, next to 72 Blackdown View, a footpath (signposted 'Norton Hillfort') goes up some steps. Just on the left, by a picnic area, there is an information board. Continue for 100 metres along the footpath to the hillfort ramparts, where there is another information board. From here go left or right, round the circuit of the ramparts, a fifteen-minute walk.

Access for disabled visitors. None.

Facilities. There is a picnic area by the car park.

Site description. Part of the site is now in the care of the Taunton Deane Borough Council and is a nature trail, while the interior of the hillfort is under cultivation and is not accessible. Excavations in 1908 and from 1968 to 1971 have shown that there was activity on the site during the Mesolithic and Neolithic periods, to judge from the flint assemblage. This was followed by an enclosure dating from the Early Bronze Age around 2000 BC. Occupation of the site continued right through the Bronze Age and into the Iron Age when a substantial rampart and ditch were constructed enclosing 5.2 hectares. The site is now much damaged and eroded, although the rampart and ditch can be clearly seen in a few places. Of particular note are three deep hollow ways which approach the hillfort on the north, south-west and south-east. Their function is uncertain, but they may indicate original entrances.

Occupation of the site seems to have continued to the Late Iron Age in the 1st century AD, and the site was later re-occupied during the Roman period in the 3rd and 4th centuries. Most hillforts seem to have been constructed in the Iron Age, but the Bronze Age origins of this site make it exceptionally important. Variants of an old proverb seem to indicate the early origins of this site:

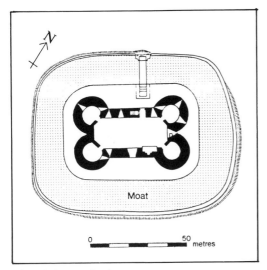

Plan of Nunney Castle.

Nertown was a market town
  when Taunton was a vuzzy down.
When Taunton was a furzy down
  Norton was a walled town.

Reading. Burrow 1924, 110, 111 (figure); Burrow 1981, 213-14; Ellis 1989; Lean 1902, 188 (on the proverbs).

Nearby sites. 11 Bishops Lydeard; 133, 134,135 Taunton.

103 NUNNEY CASTLE (Medieval castle)

Location ST 736 457. 3.5 kilometres south-west of Frome. The castle is in Nunney village, which can be reached from the Nunney Catch roundabout on the A361 road.

Parking. There is limited adjacent roadside parking and also some parking in the market square.

Access for disabled visitors. The castle is close to the road, so much of it is visible, and adjacent roadside parking is possible.

Open. Free entry at any reasonable time, but there is no access to the upper storeys.

Site description. The picturesque Medieval castle is in a style unusual for England. Nunney was essentially a fortified tower-house, built in the French style in the 1370s by Sir John de la Mare. It consists of a rectangle with round towers at each corner, about eight metres in diameter and 16.5 metres high. There were four storeys, and the

Nunney Castle, south side.

walls were 1.5-2 metres thick. The towers were surmounted by machicolated parapets and round turrets that once had conical roofs. The towers were floored at the same levels as the body of the castle, which was itself badly lit. Leland writing around 1540 said 'The Waulls be very stronge and thykke, the Stayres narrow, the Lodginge with in some what darke'. The walls linking the towers were the same height as the towers, and the building was surrounded by a deep, wide moat. Outside the moat was a 3.6 metres high curtain wall on three sides.

Sir John Poulet succeeded to the de la Mare estates in the early 15th century, and in 1577 the Poulets sold the castle to the Prater family, who had Royalist sympathies. The castle was attacked by Cromwell's forces in 1645, and a huge hole caused by cannon can be seen in the north wall. The garrison under Colonel Prater surrendered after two days, but the castle remained largely intact. On Christmas Day 1910 much of the north wall collapsed and the owner, Mr Robert Bailey-

Neale, placed the castle in the care of what is now English Heritage.

Reading. Rigold 1957.

Nearby sites. 63 Frome; 90 Marston; 92 Marston Moat; 154 Witham.

104 PEAT MOORS VISITORS CENTRE, The Willows Peat Company Garden Centre (Reconstructed prehistoric trackways and displays)

Location and parking ST 426 414. Six kilometres south of Wedmore. The visitors centre is on the road from Westhay to Shapwick at the Willows Garden Centre. It is well signposted in the vicinity. At the north end of the car park are small wooden sheds, with 'Peat Moors Visitors Centre' and 'English Heritage' signs.

Access for disabled visitors. There is good level access, and it is possible to park right outside the sheds.

Facilities. The Willows Tea Rooms, with toilets, is at the south end of the car park.

Open. Daily 9am-6pm (summer), 9am-5pm (winter).

The Museum. In the sheds there are displays on archaeology, wildlife and peat extraction through the ages in the Somerset Levels, with some artefacts, mainly prehistoric in date. Outside, there are reconstructions of Neolithic and Bronze Age trackways found in the surrounding Somerset Levels.

Reading. Coles 1982 (for trackways).

Nearby sites. 93, 94 Meare; 143, 144 Wedmore.

Penselwood, see **Ballands Castle** and **Kenwalch's Castle**.

105 PLAINSFIELD CAMP
(Iron Age hillfort)

Location and parking ST 183 362. 3.25 kilometres SSW of Nether Stowey. The hillfort is within Forestry Commission land and is also known as Cockercombe Camp. Just south of Plainsfield, past 'The Quantock Weavers', turn right (south) signposted 'Aisholt ¼, Durborough 1'. After 400 metres, turn right (west), and

after 150 metres turn right again along the unsignposted narrow tarmac road. Proceed uphill, go over the cattle grid, and after 150 metres take the right fork (not the trackway straight ahead). Follow the road through the woodland, which becomes a trackway. Turn right (the road straight ahead is gated), and there is a sign to 'Cockercombe Camp (600 metres)'. Turn left (straight ahead is gated) where there is another sign. The end of this trackway is gated, but before that point there is another sign. Park along the trackway, and walk for a few metres along the signposted path through the trees. The path comes out into open ground, and on the right is a picnic area and straight ahead is the hillfort.

Access for disabled visitors. There is only a short distance across a level path from the trackway to the hillfort, and this route has been specifically designated as suitable for disabled people by the Forestry Commission.

Facilities. A picnic area is by the hillfort.

Site description. All around the hillfort are conifer plantations, but the hillfort is clear of trees except for brambles, scrub and old tree stumps. The ramparts are largely overgrown, but are most visible by the picnic area. There are extensive views across to Bridgwater Bay and the mouth of the River Parrett. The hillfort was originally called Park Plantation, and in the early 20th century was thickly wooded, but by 1924 the whole ridge had been cleared of woodland. In 1975 the interior was recorded as again being covered by trees, but these have since been cleared. There is a single rampart and ditch enclosing 0.9 hectares, with an out-turned entrance on the east side. The hillfort is situated on a ridge of the Quantocks, with steep-sided valleys on the north-west and south-east.

Reading. Burrow 1924, 112, 113 (figure); Burrow 1981, 243-4; Grinsell 1976b, 14.

Nearby sites. 42 Crowcombe; 45 Dead Woman's Ditch; 47 Dowsborough; 101 Nether Stowey.

106 PONTER'S BALL DYKE
(Linear earthwork)

Location and parking ST 534 382 to ST 530 372. 2.5 kilometres ESE of Glastonbury Tor. The earthwork is cut by the A361 Glastonbury to

Ponter's Ball commemorative stone.

Shepton Mallet road. The raised embankment can be seen on the north of the road between Havyatt Manor and Ponters Ball bungalow, and is part of the latter's landscaped garden. Set along the pavement in the privet hedge is a 0.6 metre high commemorative stone. On the opposite side of the road the embankment can be seen between Ponters Lodge and a field. The A361 road is busy but there is a very narrow layby nearby on the minor road leading southwards to Baltonsborough.

At ST 529 379 there is a trackway (no throughway) off the A361 road by a white bungalow called 'Sunny Mead'. 175 metres to the south along this trackway, two footpaths go across the fields to another stretch of Ponter's Ball, one leading to Priory Farm and one to Kennard Moor. The old field boundaries have been removed and fences have been erected on the west side of the earthwork.

Access for disabled visitors. The earthwork is visible from the A361 road; parking is difficult.

Site description. This linear earthwork is ap-

proximately one kilometre in length. The rampart is about 9.1 metres high and 3.7 metres wide, and excavation has shown that there was a ditch on its eastern side of a similar size. It may have been an Iron Age boundary, associated with Glastonbury lake village five kilometres to the north-west, but there is a possibility of it being Dark Age in date, and associated with Glastonbury Tor. The embankment lies on elevated ground between two marshes.

It has been suggested that the name 'Ponter's Ball' may be a corruption of 'Pontis Vallum', but it has been more recently shown (McGarvie 1989) that the name is a corruption of Porter's Ball.

Reading. Burrow 1924, 134-5 (including figure); McGarvie 1989.

Nearby sites. 65, 66, 67, 69 Glastonbury.

Porlock Common, see also**Whit Stones**.

107 PORLOCK COMMON (Bronze Age stone circle and barrow)

Location and parking SS 845 446. Four kilometres south-west of Porlock. The site is on the west of the Porlock to Exford road, just north of a small bridge over a stream in the valley bottom. Parking is possible on the south-east side of the bridge. The stone circle is near a metal field gate and is marked by a metal star mounted on a metal post.

Access for disabled visitors. None.

Site description. The Bronze Age stone circle once consisted of at least ten small standing stones and eleven recumbent ones in a circle about 24.4 metres in diameter. The stones are a green micaceous sandstone. They are now in a poor condition, and very few are visible, although fourteen stones do remain – seven standing and seven fallen. A round barrow by the stone wall has been mutilated making it difficult to recognise. The site is believed to have been disturbed by military training in the Second World War, and is badly damaged. The circle was brought to Gray's attention in 1907 after it was recognised following a fire on the moor. Gray gives a full description of all the stones and a detailed plan of the stone circle and barrow.

Reading. Fowler 1988, 10; Gray 1929.

Nearby sites. 1 Alderman's Barrow; 43 Culbone Hill; 87 Madacombe; 151 Whit Stones.

Priddy, see also **Ashen Hill Barrows.**

108 PRIDDY (Bronze Age round barrow)

Location ST 527 514. 5.5 kilometres north-west of Wells. The barrow is in a pasture field 140 metres west of St. Lawrence's Church, and is visible from the field gate or from the churchyard, entered via a gate next to the school. A footpath goes across the field to the church close to the barrow.

Parking. Roadside parking is possible on the road to the church.

Access for disabled visitors. The barrow is visible from the road and from the edge of the churchyard.

Site description. This is a fairly prominent Bronze Age round barrow, situated in a field called Gill's Croft. A second barrow to the north of the church, obscured by a high hedge, was excavated by the Vicar of Priddy in 1895.

Reading. Grinsell 1971, 112.

Nearby sites. 3 Ashen Hill Barrows, 110,113 Priddy; 112 Priddy Nine Barrows.

109 PRIDDY (Bronze Age round barrow)

Location ST 521 493. Four kilometres north-west of Wells. The barrow is visible amongst trees by a Dutch barn along a trackway on the east of the road from Priddy to Wookey Hole (Pelting Drove), one kilometre south of Priddy.

Parking. There is a car park 100 metres to the south at Deer Leap, on the west of the road.

Access for disabled visitors. The barrow is visible from the road.

Site description. This Bronze Age barrow is eighteen metres in diameter and two metres high. It was planted with fir trees a short time before 1964. It may have been the 'Ramspitt Barrow near Ramspitt' where 'James Mead was whipt', mentioned in an 18th century perambulation.

Reading. Grinsell 1971, 67, 113.

Nearby sites. 57,58 Ebbor; 110 Priddy; 116 Ramspits.

110 PRIDDY (Bronze Age round barrows)

Location and parking Site 1) ST 520 522; Site 2) 522 523 (centre). 5.2 kilometres ESE of Cheddar. The site is along the B3135 (Cheddar to Green Ore) road. Parking is possible at the crossroads at ST 518 519. Site 1 consists of a round barrow in a field close to the north side of the road, nearly opposite Rowberrow Farm; Site 2 is further east opposite Hill View Farm where there are three round barrows – one at ST 521 523 covered in scrub, one beneath the field boundary, and one in the next field at ST 529 523

Access for disabled visitors. All the barrows are visible from the road.

Site description. The site consists of four Bronze Age round barrows in an area where there are many barrows, some inaccessible to the public. The one at ST 521 523 has been partly removed in the past, probably for road metalling. Further east the barrow beneath the field boundary is known as Rowbarrow, and is mentioned in an 18th century perambulation. 'Rowbarrow' is a name which has been used in the past for mounds covered in rough vegetation.

Reading. Grinsell 1971, 67, 70, 111.

Nearby sites. 3 Ashen Hill Barrows; 108, 113 Priddy; 112 Priddy Nine Barrows.

111 PRIDDY (Neolithic/Bronze Age henges)

Location and parking ST 539 525 to 542 536. Six kilometres NNW of Wells. Parking is the same as for the Ashen Hill barrows. On the north of the B3135 road is a gate to a pasture field. Traces of a low embankment marked by scrub can be seen, representing the banks of the southernmost circle, which extends east into the adjacent field.

Further east along the B3135, turn left (north) at the Miners Arms crossroads onto the B3134. At the Castle of Comfort Inn turn off this road by taking the road straight ahead as the road bends (signposted West Harptree and Bristol). On the east side is Swallet Farm Residential Training Centre (marked as Vonpitt Farm on the OS map). In the pasture field opposite, on the west of the road, the faint traces of the bank of the northernmost circle can be seen. Roadside parking is very limited.

Access for disabled visitors. Only the north-

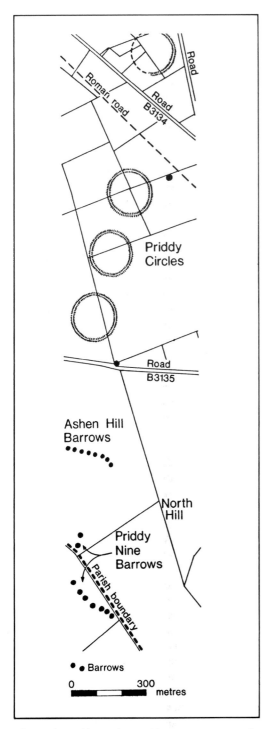

Plan of the Priddy Circles, Priddy Nine Barrows, and the Ashen Hill Barrows.

Aerial view of the Priddy Circles (the three southernmost circles) (photo by M. Aston).

ernmost circle can be seen from the roadside.

Site description. A group of three circles and a fourth circle further north are arranged in a north-south line extending over 1.2 kilometres. There is a large gap between the two north-ernmost circles as if it was intended to con-struct a fifth circle. The four circles were prob-ably ceremonial henge monuments, similar to the early form of Stonehenge, possibly dating to the Neolithic period and Bronze Age. The three northernmost circles have been damaged by lead mining. The circles had a bank and outer ditch and ranged in diameter from 160 to 172 metres. They each seem to have had a single entrance and are therefore class I henges. Excavation in the southern circle has shown that the ditches were originally U-shaped, 1-1.2 metres in depth and 3.7 metres wide. On the inner side of the ditch were two circles of large wooden posts and stakes which supported a bank of earth, turf and stones dug from the ditches. The banks were then faced by drystone walling. The wooden posts may have been up to three metres in height, projecting well above the banks.

The circles or 'rings' were visible on the ground

when Burrow (1924) was recording them, although the northernmost one was by that stage virtually obliterated. The others had banks about two metres above the level of their ditches. From the ground very little is now visible, as only slight traces of the banks and ditches survive; the site is best observed from the air.

Reading. Minnitt 1982, 27, fig. 4.1; Taylor & Tratman 1957.

Nearby sites. 3 Ashen Hill Barrows; 108,113 Priddy; 112 Priddy Nine Barrows.

112 PRIDDY NINE BARROWS
(Bronze Age round barrows)

Location and parking ST 539 515.
5.5 kilometres NNW of Wells. See Ashen Hill barrows for directions. The Priddy Nine Barrows, visible from the Ashen Hill Barrows, are situated on North Hill at a height of 307 metres OD. The footpath goes from the Ashen Hill barrows to one corner of the field where there are two barrows. Cross the gate, and the footpath follows the dry-stone wall (the parish boundary), the other side of which is a separate group of seven barrows in a curving line.

Access for disabled visitors. None.

Site description. This is a spectacular group of nine Bronze Age round barrows, over three metres in height and 45 metres in diameter. They are often confused with the Ashen Hill barrows, and were formerly called the Nine Barrows South Group. At one stage it was thought that they were called the Ashen Hill Barrows (and that the latter were the Priddy Nine Barrows). However, Grinsell has shown that these barrows have been consistently known as the Priddy Nine Barrows since 1296 (when they were known as 'Nigheberwes'). They were often mentioned in Medieval and later surveys because the parish boundary between Chewton Mendip and Priddy passed through them. 'Nine Barrows Lot' was the name of the field on the Tithe Map in which the Ashen Hill Barrows and two of the Priddy Nine Barrows group were situated. Grinsell assumes that the field was named after the southern group of barrows (the Priddy Nine Barrows), even though only two barrows of the group were in that field. On the 1" Ordnance Survey map of 1817, the southern group (Priddy

Nine Barrows) is shown as 'Nine Barrows' and the northern group (Ashen Hill Barrows) as 'Eight Barrows'.

Reading. Grinsell 1971, 67, 70, 71, 99, 113; Grinsell 1982, 103-4.

Nearby sites. 3 Ashen Hill Barrows; 108, 111,113 Priddy.

113 PRIDDY, Nine Barrows Lane
(Bronze Age round barrow)

Location ST 535 522. Six kilometres NNW of Wells. This barrow can be seen from Priddy Nine Barrows Lane and from the footpath leading from the lane to the B3135 road near the Ashen Hill barrows. It lies 300 metres south-west of Harptree Lodge.

Parking. There is some roadside parking in Nine Barrows Lane (which leads north-east from Priddy to the B3135 road at Bowery Corner), opposite a wide verge with trees.

Access for disabled visitors. The barrow can be seen from Nine Barrows Lane.

Site description. This barrow appears to be an isolated Bronze Age barrow, but is only 300 metres from the group of eight Ashen Hill barrows. It is 1.2 metres in height.

Reading. Grinsell 1971, 98.

Nearby sites. 3 Ashen Hill Barrows; 108,111 Priddy; 112 Priddy Nine Barrows.

114 RALEGH'S CROSS (Medieval cross)

Location and parking ST 038 344. Ten kilometres south-west of Williton. The cross is in landscaped grounds, by a white gate at the entrance to the car park in front of Ralegh's Cross Inn.

Access for disabled visitors. The site is accessible.

Site description. Ralegh's (or Raleigh's) Cross now consists only of a socket and shaft stump. It is of Medieval date, possibly 13th century. Various traditions surround the cross, but it seems to have been erected at the boundary of the Nettlecombe manor (then owned by the Raleghs) as a landmark on the Brendon Hills when the area was open common land crossed only by packhorses from Bampton to Watchet. It was at the junction of five

Ralegh's Cross, the cross stump.

is about 1.5 metres in height and lies in an area where there are many scattered, isolated barrows.

Reading. Grinsell 1969, 36.

Nearby sites. 37 Clatworthy Camp; 59 Elworthy Barrows; 75 Huish Champflower Barrow; 114 Ralegh's Cross.

116 RAMSPITS, Deer Leap (Deserted Medieval farmstead and field system)

Location and parking ST 515 493. Four kilometres north-west of Wells. A car park and picnic area are on the west of the road from Priddy to Wookey Hole (Pelting Drove) at ST 520 493, one kilometre south of Priddy. From the car park, cross the stile in the wall and walk towards the marker post with the arrow, and from there to the red-tiled stone building in the centre of the field (five-minute walk) where an interpretation panel is to be erected by the County Council.

Access for disabled visitors. None but there is a view of the site's landscape from the car park.

Site description. Surrounding the barn are low earthworks (turf-covered stoney banks and walls) and some walls of deserted Medieval and Post-Medieval farmsteads, enclosures and field systems, covering 26 hectares. 18 hectares of this land are owned by the County Council. The archaeological features are difficult to identify clearly, particularly as the anthills are often higher than the earthworks, and small-scale quarrying and limestone outcrops have affected the site's appearance. The site is known from documentary evidence to have been in existence by the early 14th century. It has been recently surveyed and researched by the Royal Commission on the Historical Monuments of England (Exeter).

Reading. Aston 1982, 131, fig. 13.10; Brown, Croft & Lilford 1988, 117, fig. 78.

Nearby sites. 57, 58 Ebbor; 109 Priddy; 158 Wookey Hole.

ways, only four of which now survive, and was situated to the north-west of its present position, warning travellers of a dangerous bog known as the snipe bog. It was moved across the road to its present position in the 19th century to mark the boundary between Nettlecombe (owned by the Trevelyan family) and Clatworthy (owned by the Carew family).

Reading. Siraut 1985, 113; Pooley 1877, 62-3.

Nearby sites. 37 Clatworthy Camp; 59 Elworthy Barrows; 75 Huish Champflower Barrow; 115 Ralegh's Cross.

115 RALEGH'S CROSS (Bronze Age round barrow)

Location and parking ST 041 345. 6.5 kilometres SSW of Williton. The barrow is in the field opposite Ralegh's Cross Hotel, visible from the field gate along the B3190 road. On the opposite side of the road, parking is possible next to the pub's grounds.

Disabled people access. None.

Site description. This Bronze Age round barrow

117 ROBIN HOOD'S BUTTS
(Bronze Age round barrows)

Location ST 229 143 (northern group). Nine kilometres south of Taunton. A line of barrows lies immediately south of School Farm on the west of the B3170 road, just south of the turning eastward

Robin Hood's Butts (north group).

to Fyfett. The barrows are covered in beech trees and are clearly visible from the road.

Parking. There is limited roadside parking.

Access for disabled visitors. The barrows are clearly visible from the road.

Site description. There are two groups of barrows in this area known by the name of Robin Hood's Butts. The northern group consists of five barrows so close to each other that they have almost merged into a long irregular mound, and have been mistaken for a Neolithic long barrow in the past.

The southern group of barrows is over one kilometre to the south and is more dispersed - one barrow is visible at ST 235 131 on the west of the B3135 road, and another is visible 400 metres to the south, just off the B3135 road, on the road leading westwards to Churchinford. Two other barrows have been recorded - one is inaccessible and the other has apparently been destroyed. The three surviving widely-spaced barrows barely constitute a group, but it seems that this group was originally much larger and that several barrows have been destroyed. Indeed, much folklore surrounds this southern group, including a legend that Robin Hood and Little John used to throw quoits from the barrows. The word 'Butt' means a target, mound or hillock.

It is uncertain why both groups of barrows share the same name. The confusion caused by barrows sharing the same name occurs elsewhere, as at the Priddy Nine Barrows.

Reading. Grinsell 1969, 14, 15, 37.

Nearby sites. 27 Castle Neroche; 29 Chard; 133, 136 Taunton.

Robin How, see **Joaney How.**

118 ROWBERROW (Bronze Age barrow)

Location ST 449 583. 2.5 kilometres WSW of Winscombe. Take the turning south-eastwards off the A38 road at ST 446 587, go past the church, and up to the Swan Inn. Opposite the pub is a car park for customers, from where the barrow can be seen in the adjacent field. It can also be seen (less clearly) through the hedge from the public bridleway along the lane next to the car park.

Parking. Roadside parking is very limited.

Access for disabled visitors. The barrow can be viewed from the field gate which is next to a high stone wall belonging to the Old Rectory, but roadside parking is limited.

Facilities. There are refreshments in the village.

Site description. The site is visible as a grassy mound, with some erosion on one side. It is a bowl barrow with a diameter of twenty metres and a height of two metres, and was excavated in 1813. As was normal for that time, insufficient records were kept, but the barrow seems to have covered a stone-built chamber or cist, 1.2 metres square and one metre high. Inside this chamber were a cremated burial and several grave goods, including beads, a dagger and a 'vase or cup curiously wrought'. There was an inhumation, which may have been a secondary burial but little else is known. Two Roman cinerary urns were found in 'Rowberrow Field' in 1818, and may have come from this field. The name of the barrow probably gave its name to the hamlet.

Reading. Grinsell 1971, 54, 62, 72, 118-19.

Nearby sites. 5 Axbridge; 9 Beacon Batch; 13 Black Down; 139 Tyning's Farm.

119 ROWLEY (Deserted Medieval Village)

Location and parking ST 809 582. Four kilometres west of Trowbridge. The site can be approached by a steep narrow road from Farleigh Hungerford, but access is easier from Westwood in Avon, 650 metres down the road from the National Trust's Westwood Manor. The deserted village is just south of the Somerset/Avon county border and the electricity pylons. Roadside parking is possible where there is a field gate and an overgrown track on the west and two adjacent field gates and a stile on the east. Earthworks and a hollow way can be seen in the field on the east and slight earthworks in the field on the west.

Access for disabled visitors. Part of the site can be viewed from the roadside by the field gates.

Site description. Rowley is a deserted Medieval village, which has been identified as the lost village of Wittenham, although it is referred to as Rowley from 1300. The village is first mentioned in a charter of 987, and was once an independent parish. A parish church is referred to in 1299, but was probably in existence well before that date. It was dedicated to St. Nicholas and consisted of a nave and chancel with a churchyard. The village was in decline by the late 14th century, pos-

sibly due to the Black Death or to emparking by the Hungerfords. In 1428 a licence was granted to unite the parishes of Wittenham and Farleigh Hungerford. The church and village decayed and disappeared from view, so that even its site is uncertain. The visible earthworks probably represent enclosure and house sites, and the hollow way is the remains of the original village street.

Reading. Aston & Dennison 1989, 112; Bettey 1988, 59.

Nearby sites. 60 Farleigh Hungerford; 63 Frome; 84 Kingsdown Camp; 90 Marston.

St. Michael's Hill, see **Montacute**.

Selworthy, see also **Bury Castle**.

120 SELWORTHY (Medieval cross)

Location SS 919 468. Three kilometres east of Porlock. The cross is in the east of the churchyard.

Parking. There is a car park immediately opposite the church.

Access for disabled visitors. There is a level path into the churchyard near the cross.

Facilities. Toilets are by the road on the south of the village nearly opposite the Tithe Barn. Refreshments are available in the adjacent Selworthy Green National Trust village.

Site description. The cross has three octagonal steps, a square socket with carved panelled quatrefoils, and an octagonal shaft. The head is missing.

Reading. Pooley 1877, 112.

Nearby sites. 23 Bury Castle; 73 Horner; 121 Selworthy Beacon; 148 West Luccombe.

121 SELWORTHY BEACON
(Bronze Age barrows)

Location and parking SS 921 480 to 926 478. 3.75 kilometres north-east of Porlock. On the west side of Minehead, take the road signposted to St. Michael's Church and then to North Hill. From the church, the road goes past old cottages and then emerges into open countryside. Continue for four kilometres, past an old quarry on the right (north) of the road. 250 metres further west, turn right (north) up a narrow tarmac road, and park along the road. On the right (east) is a mound close to a trackway at SS 926 478. On the other side of the road there is a mound close to the road, and further west for a distance of 400 metres there are another seven visible mounds, all covered in heather and gorse. There are no paths across the moorland.

Access for disabled visitors. Some of the barrows can be seen from the roadside.

Site description. This group of round barrows extends in a line over a distance of nearly 500 metres on the eastern slope of Selworthy Beacon. The barrows are probably all cairns, and some of them are fairly indistinct. There was probably at least one further cairn to the west on top of Selworthy Beacon, the highest point of this ridge (308 metres OD), but this spot has been used in the past as a fire beacon, and so no definite remains of cairns can be recognised.

Reading. Grinsell 1969, 19, 36, fig.1.

Nearby sites. 23 Bury Castle; 73 Horner; 120 Selworthy; 148 West Luccombe.

122 SMALL DOWN CAMP
(Iron Age hillfort)

Location ST 666 406. Five kilometres south-east of Shepton Mallet. The site is reached by a narrow steep road (Small Down Lane) from Cranmore or Chesterblade to Westcombe. Part of the hillfort can be seen from the road in a pasture field, and is partly covered by trees. There is no public access, and the barrows inside the hillfort cannot be seen from the road.

Parking. At the highest point of the hill, there is limited parking near the farm buildings.

Access for disabled visitors. The site can be partly viewed from the roadside.

Site description. This hillfort dates from the early Iron Age and is an irregular oval in shape. It was defended by two banks and ditches enclosing about two hectares, although in places there was a scarp slope instead of an outer rampart. Entrances existed on the east and south-east. Excavation has shown the ditches to have been originally six metres wide and three metres deep. About a dozen small Bronze Age barrows in a line are situated inside the hillfort and were excavated by the Rev. J. Skinner in the early 19th century and subsequently by H. St. George Gray early this cen-

Iron Age pot from Small Down Camp.

tury. In the 13th century the site was known as 'Smaledone'.

Reading. Burrow 1981, 228-9; Gray 1905.

Nearby sites. 10 Beacon Hill; 20 Bruton; 124 Spargrove; 155 Witham Friary.

123 SOUTH CADBURY CASTLE
(Iron Age and Dark Age hillfort)

Location and parking ST 628 252.

8.5 kilometres south-west of Wincanton. The site is reached from a minor road to South Cadbury south of the A303 road. There is a small layby by the church. To the south (one-minute walk) is a fairly steep lane leading to the site (five-minute walk). At the bottom of the lane, in a cottage garden, is an information board.

Access for disabled visitors. None. Parts of the site can be seen from the surrounding roads and lanes, but the whole site is only visible from some distance.

Site description. Major excavations took place at this hilltop site from 1966 to 1970. It was first occupied in the Neolithic period, from around 3300 BC, and pits of this date containing pottery and animal and human bones were found. From around 800 BC, in the Late Bronze Age, the site was reoccupied, and in the Late Iron Age, around 500 BC, the hillfort ramparts were constructed, enclosing over seven hectares. These ramparts were modified on several occasions, resulting in a multivallate hillfort with four massive earthen banks and accompanying ditches. There were entrances in the south-west, north-east (the main approach today), and the east. Inside the hillfort

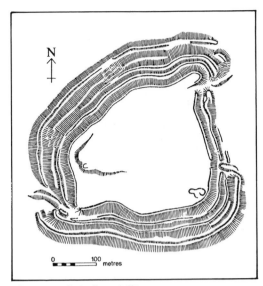

Plan of South Cadbury hillfort.

were several buildings of Iron Age date, including a bronzesmith's workshop, a small square cella or temple, and circular huts, as well as large storage pits.

Occupation continued into the Roman period, but in about AD 70 the site was attacked by the Romans, leaving evidence of a massacre with bodies of adults and children. At the same time, the south-west gate was burnt down, and the ramparts were slighted. Between AD 400-600, in the Dark Ages, a new rampart was built on the innermost Iron Age rampart, using a timber framework. Amongst the evidence for this period was a large rectangular timber hall, and also pottery imported from the Mediterranean. Legend associates this period of occupation with Arthur, and 16th century topographers identified the site as Camelot, the court of Arthur. Occupation continued to the 7th century.

In the late Saxon period, the hilltop was again defended when it became a burh or fortified town for a short period during the reign of King Ethelred. Coins were minted here as an emergency measure between AD 1010 and 1020. The burh was defended by a mortared stone wall 1.2 metres wide, built around the whole hilltop site.

Surviving visible remains of the hillfort are the well-preserved ramparts, the perimeter of which can be walked. There is a model of the site in the Museum of South Somerset, Yeovil.

Reading. Alcock 1972; Burrow 1981, 94-5, 134-8, 210-11.

Nearby sites. 89 Maperton; 91 Marston Magna; 100 Nether Adber; 147 West Camel.

124 SPARGROVE (Medieval moat)

Location ST 670 378. Three kilometres north-west of Bruton. The site is reached via the B3081 Bruton to Evercreech road. There is roadside parking near a little bridge over the stream. Immediately south of the bridge, on the west of the road, is a footpath (not signposted). Go through the barbed wire fence where it is sheathed in plastic, up the grassy bank, and across the field. On the left is a derelict barn. The footpath leads towards the buildings in the distance (Spargrove Farm), near which is a substantial bank running east-west which belongs to the moat. Follow the footpath the length of the bank, and nearly at the corner of the field, the bank turns a right-angle southwards.

Access for disabled visitors. None.

Site description. The east-west embankment is part of a moated site with a rectangular moat and an outer bank. The bank survives to a height of 1.8 metres, but part of the site has been levelled. The moated site is of Medieval date, although the present farmhouse and buildings are later in date (16th-17th century). Just to the south, a church of St. Lawrence is known to have existed by 1191 when it is mentioned in a papal bull as 'Capella de Sperkegrave'. By 1718 the chapel had been demolished, and nothing is now visible. A short distance to the east, there is a hollow way and earthworks of a deserted Medieval village, probably contemporary with the moated site, but these remains are inaccessible to visitors.

Reading. Aston 1982, 130, 133.

Nearby sites. 20 Bruton; 26 Castle Cary; 36 Clanville; 122 Small Down Camp.

125 SPAXTON (Medieval cross)

Location ST 225 370. Six kilometres west of Bridgwater. Travelling from Bridgwater along the Spaxton road, go past Four Forks. 500 metres further on, turn right (north) into Splatt Lane,

Stavordale Priory from the South-west.

signposted to Spaxton church. St. Margaret's church is 200 metres further north on the left (west), and the cross is in the churchyard by the south porch of the church.

Parking. There is limited parking by the church in Splatt Lane or in the adjacent Church Road.

Access for disabled visitors. There is limited parking in Church Road, from where there is level access to the cross through the gate at the south-west corner of the churchyard.

Site description. The cross consists of three octagonal steps, an octagonal socket with carved shields on each face, and an octagonal shaft. There is a solid rectangular head with relief carving on each side. The carvings are difficult to see as they are covered in lichen. The cross is of 14th century date.

Reading. Pooley 1877, 149-50.

Nearby sites. 62 Fiddington; 101 Nether Stowey; 105 Plainsfield Camp; 127 Stogursey.

126 STAVORDALE PRIORY
(Medieval priory)

Location ST 736 320. Six kilometres south-east of Bruton. At Charlton Musgrove turn east into Barrow Lane where there is a row of houses on the left, one with a Post Office. When the road bears left, turn right up a narrow no-through lane (at ST 731 318). Go past Stavordale Stud on the right, and 200 metres further on is a private house, converted from the priory. There is no access, but the house is visible from the road.

Parking. There is limited roadside parking.

Access for disabled visitors. The priory site is visible from the road.

Site description. The exact date of the foundation of this small Augustinian priory is not known, but it was probably founded in the 12th century. It is also not known why it was founded so close to Bruton which had its own priory of the same order. First mention of it is in 1243 when Roger

Tyrel and his wife are named as benefactors. The priory buildings fell into decay, but an endowment enabled rebuilding to take place from 1439 to 1443. The priory still suffered from poverty and was in such a bad state that it was taken over by Taunton Priory in 1533. In 1536 the Zouche family wrote to Thomas Cromwell to try to obtain Stavordale as their private residence on the grounds that it had been founded by their family. The priory was surrendered to the Crown on 12 February 1539 along with Taunton Priory, and by 1548 the Zouche family was living there. The priory church still survives, converted into a private house and is still recognisable as a monastic building.

Reading. Bates 1905 (the frontispiece shows a photograph of the building before its more recent restoration); Colt Hoare 1824, 103-51; Scott Holmes 1911, 139-41.

Nearby sites. 6 Balland's Castle; 20 Bruton; 82 Kenwalch's Castle; 89 Maperton.

127 STOGURSEY (Medieval castle, cross and well)

Location ST 203 425. Ten kilometres northwest of Bridgwater. From the High Street, turn southwards into Castle Street, and there is a footpath on the right (west), which goes over a stile and runs alongside a private trackway. The footpath goes round the east and south sides of the castle moat.

Parking. There is room to park in the High Street.

Access for disabled visitors. None.

Site description. The well-preserved stone walls of the castle keep are visible on a mound from outside the moat. Also visible is a small house which was built into the ruins at the position of the gatehouse and which has been recently restored by the Landmark Trust and converted to a holiday home. The bailey earthworks, situated in the orchard to the east, are visible from the little bridge by the moat.

Stogursey castle is first mentioned in 1090 when it may have been owned by the de Courcy family. It was held for King John in 1215, and was ordered to be destroyed in the following year. This does not seem to have been done as a further order

was made for it to be destroyed a few years later, which was also ignored. The castle had a stone curtain wall with towers and an inner and outer bailey. The castle passed into the possession of Sir Robert Fitzpaine. It was burnt down in 1457 during the Wars of the Roses, and has remained in ruins ever since.

In St. Andrews Road there is a cross shaft, and nearby is St. Andrews well, possibly an important holy well in the Medieval period. The archway to the well was built in 1757, and the site has been recently restored.

Reading. Aston & Leech 1977, 131-3, pl. 10, maps 56, 57; Burrow 1924, 128, 129 (figure).

Nearby sites. 62 Fiddington; 85 Lilstock; 101 Nether Stowey; 152 Wick Barrow.

128 STOKE-SUB-HAMDON (Medieval college buildings of the Beauchamp chantry)

Location ST 473 175. 1.75 kilometres SSE of Martock. The buildings are on the west side of North Street, through a large archway. A small old National Trust sign on the wall along the road marks the property, now known as 'The Priory'.

Parking. There is limited parking by the memorial hall in nearby West Street, or very limited roadside parking outside the property. There is a car park at a distance of a two-minute walk by the Half Moon Inn on the road to Ham Hill.

Access for disabled visitors. Parking is possible outside, and there is access to the courtyard areas (grass-covered with gravel paths) as far as the field gate. Three steps lead up to the hall. Toilets are by the memorial hall in West Street.

Facilities. There are shops and refreshments in the village, and toilets as above.

Site description. Wealthy people sometimes gave endowments to establish a college of priests to serve in a private chapel or parish church, and to devote their time to prayer for the founder and his descendants. These chantry foundations were not monasteries but were specially designed religious houses, and one was established at Stoke in the 1304.

By the late 12th century the Beauchamp family held the manor of Stoke, and in 1333 permission was obtained to crenellate the manor house. The

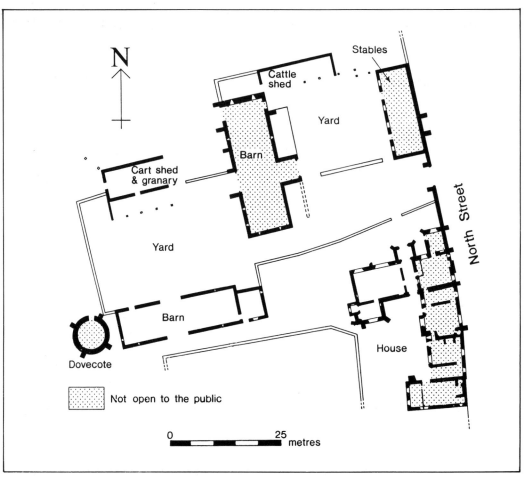

Plan of the Medieval collegiate buildings at Stoke-sub-Hamdon.

fortified manor house was known as Beauchamp Castle and was in the area of the present-day Castle Street and Castle Farm, although nothing is now visible. The chapel of St. Nicholas stood in the courtyard of the manor house, and had been existence since at least 1283. In 1304 the Beauchamp family established a collegiate chantry attached to St. Nicholas chapel. There were five chaplains, one of whom was provost, and they were housed in North Street, 200 metres northeast of the manor house enclosure.

The male line of the Beauchamp family died out in the 14th century when John Beauchamp died childless in 1361, and the manor house was allowed to fall into ruins. The chantry continued as it had an independent endowment, but it suffered from poverty and quarrels. In 1444 Bishop Thomas Bekynton suspended the provost for bad management and ordered the repair and restoration of the college buildings, but by the mid 16th century they were described by John Leland as being 'yn Decay'. He also described the manor house: 'I saw at Stoke in a Botom hard by the Village very notable Ruines of a greate Manor Place or Castelle, and yn this Maner Place remaynith a very auncient Chapelle'.

The chantry survived the Dissolution of the Monasteries, although being financially impoverished it seems that the college buildings were by then leased to a farmer. However, in 1548 under Edward VI the chantry was suppressed, its endowments seized, and the chapel of St. Nicholas

Stoke-sub-Hamdon dovecote.

was demolished. The chaplains' lodging house continued to be leased, mainly to farmers, up to recent times. In 1946 the buildings were purchased by the National Trust. Part of one of the buildings is privately tenanted. The buildings consist of a house, barns and dovecote dating from the chantry foundation in 1304.

Go through the large archway (with a smaller blocked gateway to its north) into the courtyard where there is an information board. In front is a large thatched barn, and to the left (south) is the house which consists of three unequal wings, much of which was restored by the National Trust in 1967-8. The barns have been altered but are Medieval in origin. The hall range is the oldest part of the building and can be visited by going up three steps, into the passageway and then into the first room on the right (where there are guidebooks for sale). The hall was 8.5 metres x 5.5 metres and was the 14th century refectory-living room of the college, and displays evidence for several phases of building including Bekynton's 15th century repair work. The hall was originally open to the roof, but a floor was inserted in the 17th century and has since been removed.

From the hall, a door leads into another room (the bay) which was also originally open to the roof. The floor (since removed) together with the still visible fireplaces were also inserted in the 17th century. Both rooms have earth and stone floors. The rest of the house is not accessible to visitors.

Back in the courtyard, to the north of the archway, there is a stable building with a modern thatched roof. Cross the courtyard and go through the field gate. On the left (south) are the remains of a barn which was badly damaged by a fire in 1969. Opposite, by the large barn, is another smaller barn, possibly a cartshed. Adjoining the fire-damaged barn are the remains of the lower part of a dovecote, inside which the nesting boxes for 500 pigeons can be seen. The dovecote is currently roofless, but was still roofed in the 19th century. Between the large barn and the stables is an open-fronted 19th century farm building.

Reading. Leaflet on the Priory, 1979, produced by the National Trust (authors of various sections being P.M. Ireland and J.E.C. Peters); Leach 1980 (on excavations at the associated castle site in 1976); Scott Holmes 1911, 161-2.

Nearby sites. 25 Cart Gate; 72 Ham Hill; 97 Montacute; 153 Witcombe.

129 STOWELL (Deserted Medieval Village)

Location ST 683 219. 3.5 kilometres NNE of Milborne Port. One kilometre north-west of Templecombe, take the turning on the left (west) of the A357, signposted to Milborne Wick. Follow this road for 2.5 kilometres, past Stowell Farm and an isolated church on the left. After 350 metres the road bears right (west). On the left (south) is a track leading over the railway, near which are Clare Cottages. On the north of the road is Clare Farm. The field between Clare Cottages and the road (to the south of the farm) contains earthworks.

Parking. There is a wide entrance to the track-way over the railway.

Access for disabled visitors. The site is visible from the road.

Site description. The clearly visible earthworks near Clare Farm seem to represent enclosures and house platforms. These probably mark the site of a deserted Medieval village, of which only the farm has survived to the present day.

Nearby sites. 74 Horsington; 89 Maperton; 91 Marston Magna; 123 South Cadbury Castle.

130 STREET (The Shoe Museum)

Location ST 484 367. The museum is at the east end of Street in the oldest part of the C & J Clark Shoe Factory. The entrance is in the High Street, opposite the Bear Hotel, just beyond Wilfrid Road.

Parking. Roadside parking is possible, or pay car parks are situated nearby.

Access for disabled visitors. None.

Facilities. There is a sales area. Refreshments, shops, banks and toilets are in the town.

Open. Easter Monday to 31 October, Monday-Friday 10am-4.45pm, Saturday 10am-4.30pm. During winter months by appointment only. Parties should book in advance.

The Museum. The museum has an extensive collection of shoes of all periods, dating from the Roman period, although not related to Somerset's archaeology.

Nearby sites. 65, 66, 67, 69 Glastonbury.

131 SWEETWORTHY (Iron Age hillfort)

Location and parking SS 890 425. Four kilometres south of Porlock. Sweetworthy can be approached from various directions, including from Dunkery Beacon, using paths on National Trust land. The shortest route is from near Cloutsham. On the south of the road from Cloutsham to Luccombe, there is a large signposted National Trust car park in a meadow by a stream (East Water) at SS 894 430, a short distance east of Cloutsham Farm, just past a hairpin bend.

From here, turn left and walk westwards along the road for thirty metres, past a small footbridge on the left (south). Thirty metres further on, there is a narrow unsignposted path through bracken and nettles to the old ford (five metres distance). This path can be difficult to find. Cross the ford by the rough stepping stones, and go uphill through woodland. After a few metres, the worn path bears right and continues uphill. 200 metres from the

ford, there is a fence with a gate on the right. The path continues uphill, parallel with the fence, and with the steep-sided valley of Aller Combe on the left, coming out into open moorland after a further 180 metres. Turn right and the enclosure earthworks can be seen in the adjacent field, just north of a line of beech trees.

Alternatively, at the fence, go through the gate and follow the grassy path through gorse, bracken and trees. After 150 metres, there is a fence with a stile. The earthworks are at the top of the field.

Access for disabled visitors. None.

Facilities. There is a picnic area in the car park.

Site description. The hillfort or enclosure of Sweetworthy is on a north-facing slope of Dunkery Hill at 305 metres OD. It is defended by a single rampart and external ditch enclosing 0.25 hectares, with steep-sided valleys on the east and north. The rampart is still very prominent, and the ditch is visible in places, particularly on the east side where it is used as a trackway.

Reading. Burrow 1981, 257; Grinsell 1970, 79, 85.

Nearby sites. 28 Chapel Cross; 49 Dunkery Beacon; 70 Great Rowbarrow and Little Rowbarrow; 81 Joaney How and Robin How.

132 TARR STEPS (Clapper bridge)

Location and parking SS 867 321. Six kilometres north-west of Dulverton. Take the turning at the crossroads by the Caratacus stone (Spire Cross) signposted 'Tarr Steps (Ancient Monument)'. Follow this narrow road downhill for two kilometres to a large pay car park on the left. Continue on foot down the road for 500 metres or take the signposted scenic route.

Access for disabled visitors. Parking is possible close to the steps by continuing down the road past the car park, but can be very congested in the tourist season.

Facilities. There are toilets in the car park.

Site description. At the bottom of the valley, crossing the River Barle, is a clapper bridge formed from stone slabs. The bridge is fifty-five metres long and 1.5 metres wide, with seventeen spans. The covering stones are about 0.15 metres thick. The bridge has been described as Bronze Age in date, but it is thought more likely to be Medieval.

Tarr Steps in winter.

It was obviously built as a packhorse bridge and for foot traffic. From time to time the bridge has been rebuilt after being damaged or washed away by floods, including after the 1948 and 1952 floods, when the stones were lifted back into position using cranes. Another name for the bridge was the Devil's Bridge.

Reading. Grinsell 1970, 148-50.

Nearby sites. 24 Caratacus Stone; 71 Green Barrow and Brightworthy Barrows; 141 Wambarrows; 156 Withypool.

133 TAUNTON (County Museum)

Location ST 226 246. The museum is in the castle. Tel. Taunton (0823) 255504. For directions and parking see Taunton Castle (134).

Access for disabled visitors. Access is only possible to part of the ground floor (the Great Hall). There is no access to the archaeology gallery. See Taunton Castle (134) for parking and toilets.

Facilities. There are toilets and a sales area in the museum. Refreshments, banks and shops are in the town.

Admission charge. A charge is made. Free to members of Somerset Archaeology and Natural History Society, Friends of Taunton Castle and

Taunton County Museum, reconstruction of an Iron Age loom.

Friends of the Abbey Barn.

Open. All year, 10am-5pm, Monday to Saturday apart from 25 and 26 December and 1 January.

The Museum. There are several displays on archaeology, natural history, geology, art and local history. The archaeology displays range from the Palaeolithic to the Medieval period, and include a model of the Bronze Age Wick Barrow, a prehis-

The Iron Age dugout canoe, found near Shapwick in 1916, and now in the Castle Museum.

toric wooden trackway from the Somerset Levels, a hoard of Bronze Age bronze artefacts from Stogursey, a prehistoric wooden dugout canoe from Shapwick, a model of an Iron Age house from Glastonbury Lake Village, Roman finds from Charterhouse, finds from Taunton Castle, a Roman skeleton from Ilchester, and a Roman mosaic from the Low Ham villa. There is also a display on Harold St. George Gray who was prominent for so long in Somerset's archaeology.

Nearby sites. 102 Norton Fitzwarren; 134, 135, 136 Taunton.

134 TAUNTON (Medieval castle)

Location ST 225 246. The site of the castle is in the town centre within the Castle Green area. The main areas visible are the east gate (Castle Bow) next to the Castle Hotel, reached from Castle Green or Fore Street, and part of the Inner Ward, reached from Castle Green.

Parking. There are several pay car parks in the town, the closest (and most expensive) being the Castle Green car park, reached from Castle Way near the old cinema (now a bingo club).

Access for disabled visitors. There is fairly level access to the visible remains, although some paths are cobbled. There are toilets on the east side of Castle Green car park (male) and in Castle Walk (female). Access is possible to the Great Hall (part of the museum), and parking is possible outside the museum entrance, although there is a height limit of seven feet under the portcullis.

Facilities. There are toilets (female in Castle Walk near Castle Bow; male in Castle Green car park). Shops, banks and refreshments are available in the town. See also Taunton Museum.

Admission charge. There is a charge to the museum.

Open. There is access at all times except to the museum.

Site description. Beneath the site of the present castle and Castle Green is evidence for a Saxon cemetery, possibly belonging to the Saxon minster church founded in the 8th century. The land was part of a large estate owned by the Bishops of Winchester, who in 1138 had a castle built on the site. It consisted of the rectangular tower of a great keep, part of the foundations of which can be seen in the gardens used by the Castle Hotel (which was built adjoining the castle's East Gate).

From the 12th-13th centuries the castle underwent various phases of development by successive bishops of Winchester. This work included the construction of the Inner Ward (or bailey) round the keep, comprising various offices and domestic buildings. The Outer Ward of the castle was surrounded by a moat (part of which followed the line of Corporation Street before turning northwards parallel to Fore Street and North Street). There was also an East Gate (now known as Castle Bow), a West Gate and a Watergate, and various buildings such as a dovecote, barns, granaries and stables. The Outer Ward is now known as Castle Green.

The Medieval castle required constant repair and was liable to flooding, although its defences were rarely put to the test. In 1551 the castle and manor were exchanged by the bishop of Winchester with Edward VI for other lands. By 1635 the castle was in a state of disrepair but was refortified with the outbreak of Civil War in 1642. Royalist forces took the castle and remained in control for a year until 5 June 1644 when the castle changed hands following a week's siege by Roundhead forces under Robert Blake. He himself was subsequently besieged from August 1644 until 11 May 1645 when the Royalist forces withdrew to Bridgwater. In 1662 Charles II ordered the castle keep to be demolished, and by the late 18th century the other castle buildings were in

Taunton, entrance to castle (inner ward).

a poor state, but underwent restoration. However in the late 19th century parts of the castle began to be destroyed, and so they were purchased by the Somerset Archaeological and Natural History Society in 1874. Even then, the society did not have the same standards of preservation as today, and much was altered, refurbished or even demolished (probably including part of the keep). These buildings now house the society's offices and library, the local history library, and the County Museum.

Reading. Bush 1988. All the following useful papers are published within Leach (ed.) 1984: Burrow 1984; Bush & Meek 1984; Clements 1984; Leach & Pearson 1984; Pearson 1984; Rodwell 1984; see also the section on finds (pp. 133ff.).

Nearby sites. 102 Norton Fitzwarren; 133, 135, 136 Taunton.

Taunton, Priory Barn.

135 TAUNTON, Priory Barn (Museum and Medieval priory building)

Location and parking ST 228 249. The site is near St. James' Church in Taunton. There is a pedestrian entrance off Priory Avenue. Entrance is also from the County Cricket Ground off Priory Bridge Road (except during First Class Cricket Matches), opposite a public car park, by the corner of St. Augustine Street, next to The Church Organ Works. There is parking in the cricket ground. From the car park, turn left (signposted 'Old Pavilion'), then left again by the shop. Tel. Secretary: Taunton (0823) 275893.

Access for disabled visitors. Level access is possible from the cricket ground car park.

Facilities. There are refreshments in the cricket pavilion, and toilets near the museum by the shop. Shops, banks, refreshments and toilets are also available in the town.

Admission charge. There is a small charge.

Open. Monday-Saturday 10am-4pm but ring to confirm October to March.

Site description. The Somerset Cricket Museum is housed in a building now known as 'Priory Barn'. Throughout its life the building has had many alterations, but it is basically a late 15th or early 16th century two-storied building. It is composed of mortared stone walls standing at least five metres high and with a thickness of 0.7 metres. The building was probably part of the priory at Taunton, and may have been a gatehouse or lodging house. On the south end there are indications of a previous archway through to the priory. The building has been recently renovated, and archaeological finds from the excavation are on display.

Ivory knife handle found c. 1812 on the site of Taunton Priory.

Seal of Taunton Priory.

The Augustinian Priory of SS. Peter and Paul was founded in 1198 on land given by Henry of Blois, Bishop of Winchester. It was dissolved in 1539, and the site was thoroughly destroyed. As a result, very little is known of the priory's layout and buildings. Apart from street names in the vicinity, Priory Barn is the only visible presence of the former priory. Grassy hillocks could be seen on the priory site in the late 19th century, but that area is now built over. When the area was redeveloped for housing at the end of the 19th century, massive foundations were apparently found, but the exact position of the priory is still not known.

Reading. Bush 1984; Hinchliffe 1984; Leach 1984; Scott Holmes 1911, 141-4; see also the sections on finds in Leach (ed) 1984 (pp. 134ff.)

Nearby sites. 102 Norton Fitzwarren; 133, 134, 136 Taunton.

136 TAUNTON, St. Margaret's Leper Hospital (Medieval hospital)

Location ST 238 247. The building is situated on a triangular island at the junction of Hamilton Road and Leycroft Road, near the traffic lights at the junction of East Reach and Lisieux Way.

Parking. Roadside parking is possible in Leycroft Road.

Access for disabled visitors. There is level access to the exterior of the building and adjacent parking.

Facilities. Toilets, shops, banks and refreshments are available in Taunton.

Site description. St. Margaret's Hospital is a long low thatched building with what appears to be an inn sign (actually a Rural Community Council sign) on its south side. The building stands isolated on a triangular green in a housing estate. It was originally outside the town of Taunton, and was founded around 1185 as the Hospital of the Holy Ghost and St. Margaret, and was a lazar house for the care of lepers. Around this building there was a complex of other buildings, including barns, a cemetery and a chapel. St. Margaret's was apparently burnt down in the early 16th century and was rebuilt by the Abbot of Glastonbury. During the Dissolution of the Monasteries, land and the chapel were sold off, but the

Taunton, St Margaret's Hospital.

building seemed to continue in use as almshouses with seven residents, and was used as such until the present century. By 1936 the building was threatened with demolition, being considered unfit for human habitation, but the building was saved and it is now used by the Community Council for Somerset, and as a Rural Crafts Centre.

Reading. Byford 1987, 113; Hugo 1874; Pevsner 1958a, 317-18.

Nearby sites. 102 Norton Fitzwarren; 133, 134, 135 Taunton.

137 TRENDLE RING, Bicknoller
(Iron Age hillfort)

Location and parking ST 118 393. Four kilometres south-east of Williton. The enclosure can be best seen on the hillside above the new houses from the large layby west of Bicknoller on the A358 road at ST 106 392.

Access for disabled visitors. The site can be seen from the A358 layby.

Site description. Trendle or Trundle Ring is situated on a steep hillside on the edge of a wooded valley and can be clearly seen from a distance. It is a small, roughly circular hillfort or enclosure covering 0.8 hectares at 170 metres OD. It is defended by a bank and ditch, with a simple entrance on the east side. The name 'Trendle' means circle.

Reading. Burrow 1924, 102, 103 (figure); Burrow 1981, 249; Grinsell 1976b, 18

Nearby sites. 7 Battlegore; 42 Crowcombe; 45 Dead Woman's Ditch; 47 Dowsborough.

138 TWO BARROWS (Bronze Age round barrows)

Location SS 747 362. 3.75 kilometres south-west of Simonsbath. At the Kinsford Gate crossroads (at SS 739 366), on the Devon/Somerset border, turn south-eastwards (signposted to Sandyway and Molland). Go uphill along the road through enclosed moorland, and after 550 metres a round barrow is on the right (in Devon). After a further 200 metres there is a low barrow on top of the hill on the right of the road (in Devon), while on the left (in Somerset) a substantial barrow can be seen. Go through a small wooden gate with a sign 'Exmoor National Park viewpoint private land - access by courtesy of owner. Public enter at own risk.' Right in front is the substantial barrow approximately three metres high and with a hollow in the centre. The surrounding land is boggy. About thirty metres to the west, right by the field boundary along the

Tyning's Farm, Bronze Age barrows.

road, is another mound about one metre high. 100 metres east of the large barrow is another low mound covered in reeds.

Parking. There is roadside parking just to the south-east of the field gate.

Access for disabled visitors. The large barrow can be seen clearly from the roadside.

Site description. The three round barrows in Somerset and the adjacent round barrow across the Devon border form a group known as 'Two Barrows'. The name probably relates to the two barrows right on the county border which are likely to have been used as boundary markers. The four barrows are in an east-west line on the top of a ridge overlooking the surrounding landscape.

Reading. Grinsell 1969, 33; Grinsell 1970, 60, 154, fig. 5.

Nearby sites. 15 Blue Gate; 41 Cow Castle; 71 Green Barrow and Brightworthy Barrows; 141 Wambarrows.

139 TYNING'S FARM (Bronze Age round barrows)

Location ST 469 563. 2.75 kilometres NNE of Cheddar. The barrows are situated east of the road from Shipham to Charterhouse, visible in a pasture field south of Tyning's Farm, to the south and east of the road (at a right-angle bend).

Parking. Roadside parking is possible.

Access for disabled visitors. The barrows are visible from the roadside.

Site description. Five barrows close to Tyning's Farm probably formed part of a Bronze Age cemetery. Three prominent mounds are in a line close to the road. There is another mound just visible further east, but this is poorly preserved, and a fifth barrow is in the field to the west. The barrows have been excavated and contained Early Bronze Age cremations, one in a stone cist.

Reading. Grinsell 1971, 96; Read 1924; Taylor 1933; Taylor 1951 (on the excavation of the southernmost barrow).

Nearby sites. 9 Beacon Batch; 13 Black Down; 35 Cheddar Gorge; 118 Rowberrow.

Upton, St. James church tower.

140 UPTON, St. James' Church
(Medieval church)

Location SS 980 294. 6.5 kilometres ENE of Dulverton. Just west of Upton, take the road northwards, signposted to Brompton Regis. After 275 metres, turn left into the no-through road, signposted 'Upton Farm 1m'. At the end of this single-track road, by the entrance to Upton Farm, the church is in a field to the left (south-west), entered by a small wooden gate.

Parking. Extremely limited in this single-track road, and access to the farm must be kept clear.

Access for disabled visitors. The church can be viewed from the field gate.

Site description. Only the west tower and the lower courses of the nave and chancel walls survive of the former parish church of St. James, Upton. The church was built in the early 14th century, but in 1867 a new church was built closer to the main population of the village, and the old church fell into decay. Many of the fittings were dispersed, but the bells and font were moved to the new church. After a century of neglect and decay, the remains of the church passed into the care of the redundant churches fund in 1973.

It is possible to enter the tower, and inside on the wall is a very worn 17th century tombstone. Near the church ruins is a partially buried socket stone of an old cross. Elsewhere in the field are the remains of gravestones and low mounds of numerous burials. Around the field is a bank, possibly the perimeter wall of the former graveyard.

Reading. Pevsner 1958a, 326.

Nearby sites. 37 Clatworthy Camp; 75 Huish Champflower Barrow; 114 Ralegh's Cross; 157 Wiveliscombe Barrow.

141 WAMBARROWS, Winsford Hill
(Bronze Age round barrows)

Location and parking SS 876 343. 7.25 kilometres north-west of Dulverton. Going north-west along the B3223 road from Spire Cross, there is a car park on the right (north) of the road, from where one barrow is visible. Further north along the road is a layby close to the stone pillar with a National Trust sign marking Winsford Hill. At this point there are three further barrows known as Wambarrows.

Access for disabled visitors. The barrows (in particular the Wambarrows) are clearly visible from the road.

Site description. The prominent Bronze Age round barrows known as Wambarrows are close together in a line. They vary from 0.9 metres to 1.5 metres in height, and are situated on the highest point (426 metres OD) of Winsford Hill, on National Trust land. They were mentioned in perambulations of Exmoor in 1219 and 1279, when they were used as boundary markers. They were known as 'Wamburg' in 1219, but by 1279 they were called 'Wambureghe'. The largest barrow is surrounded by a fence. All three have concavities in the top indicating that they have been dug into in the past, apparently at the beginning of this century or earlier. The locality is allegedly haunted by the Black Dog which is said to be guarding treasure.

Reading. Grinsell 1969, 13, 14, 41-2; Grinsell 1976a, 103.

Nearby sites. 15 Blue Gate; 41 Cow Castle; 71 Green Barrow and Brightworthy Barrows; 138 Two Barrows.

Washford, see **Cleeve Abbey, Washford**.

Watchet, see also **Daw's Castle, Watchet**.

142 WATCHET, Market House Museum

Location ST 069 434. Market House, Market Street, Watchet, near the harbour slipway. Tel. Secretary: Minehead (0643) 7132, or the curator: Watchet (0984) 31209.

Parking. There is a pay car park nearly opposite the museum (off Market Street) and another one off Swain Street.

Access for disabled visitors. The museum is on one level floor but access is only possible if the two large steps at the entrance can be negotiated. There are toilets in the car park off Swain Street.

Facilities. There are refreshments and shops in the town, toilets at the harbour and in the car park off Swain Street, and a sales area in the museum.

Admission charge. There is a small charge.

Open. Easter, and from mid-May to the end of September, daily 10.30am-12.30pm, 2.30pm-4.30pm. Also 7pm-9pm at Easter, July and August. Parties by arrangement.

The Museum. There are displays of archaeological finds, and in particular finds from Roman sites in the district, and prehistoric flintwork, including Palaeolithic handaxes from Doniford. There is also a display on the Saxon coin mint at Watchet, illustrated mainly by replica coins.

Nearby sites. 7 Battlegore; 38 Cleeve Abbey; 44 Daw's Castle; 137 Trendle Ring.

143 WEDMORE (Medieval cross)

Location ST 435 479. In the south-east corner of the churchyard of St. Mary Magdalene Church, in Church Street.

Parking. There is a short-stay shopper's car park in 'The Borough' or limited roadside parking by the church.

Access for disabled visitors. The churchyard can be entered at the west end, nearly opposite Glanville Road.

Facilities. There are toilets near the car park entrance in The Borough, and shops, refreshments and banks in the town.

Site description. The cross once stood near the west porch but was moved in the early 19th cen-

Medieval cross in the churchyard, Wedmore.

tury. The shaft is a square tapering monolith or-
namented with recessed canopied niches on each
face. It is mounted on three circular steps and a
socket. The top of the shaft has been recently restored, and there is a spherical head which was
restored in the late 19th century. In the north-west
corner of the churchyard is a stone set up in 1878
to commemorate King Alfred and the 1,000th an-
niversary of the Peace of Wedmore which resulted
from Alfred's defeat of the Danes.

Reading. Pooley 1877, 113-14.

Nearby sites. 34 Cheddar; 35 Cheddar Gorge;
94 Meare; 144 Wedmore.

144 WEDMORE (Medieval village cross)

Location ST 436 478. Situated on the east side
of the street known as 'The Borough', near Ler-
burne House, and south of The Borough Mall. It is
in a small enclosure with a wrought iron gate and
railings. There is an information panel on a wall.

Parking. A short stay shoppers car park is in The
Borough Mall, or else limited roadside parking.

Access for disabled visitors. The cross is
visible from the roadside.

Facilities. There are toilets near the car park
entrance in The Borough, and refreshments, shops
and banks in the town.

Site description. The cross consists of one
square step, a square socket, an octagonal shaft,
and a much damaged and weathered head. Pooley
described it as 'one of the nearly perfect Crosses
that have escaped destruction'. The canopied head
contained sculptures on all four sides with a
pyramidal central spire rising from the canopy.
The cross is of late 14th century date, and
originally stood in the village by the shambles.

Reading. Pooley 1877, 114-15.

Nearby sites. 34 Cheddar; 35 Cheddar Gorge;
94 Meare; 143 Wedmore.

145 WELLS (Cathedral)

Location and parking ST 551 458. There are
several pay car parks in Wells (including those off
Chamberlain Street and Princes Road). The closest
is in the market square (off Sadler Street) which
becomes very congested and is closed on market

days (Wednesday and Saturday). The cathedral is
on the east side of the city, and can be reached on
foot from the market square through Penniless
Porch, or through the gateway in Sadler Street
which leads into Cathedral Green. Cathedral
Secretary, West Cloister Offices, Wells, BA5 2PA.
Tel. Wells (0749) 674483.

Access for disabled visitors. There is parking
in Cathedral Green, and a ramp gives access to the
west front. The cathedral should be entered by the
north-west door in the west front (where there is a
noticeboard about access). There is level access to
much of the cathedral, but not to the archaeology
display. A Radar toilet is available – ask a virger,
the shop or restaurant for the key. There is access
to the shop and restaurant in the West Cloister
which is reached by going out of the north-west
door, turning left, and entering the entrance to the
cloister.

Facilities. A shop and restaurant are in the West
Cloister. Toilets are reached from the East Cloister
by the Camery. Banks, shops, toilets and refreshments are also available in the City. Concerts and
services are held in the cathedral. There is an information desk in the north transept.

Admission charge. Donations are invited for
the maintenance of the cathedral. There is a small
charge for viewing the library.

Open. The cathedral is open at all times, and the
library can be viewed from 2.30pm in the summer.

Site description. Wells Cathedral has a very
long and complex history, with a great deal to see
for the visitor. Christian activity on the site dates
from the end of the Roman period, with a mortuary chapel and cemetery. From the 8th century there was a Saxon minster church dedicated
to St. Andrew. In 909 it was elevated to the
status of cathedral, and the church was probably situated beneath the present cloister. A new
cathedral began to be constructed from about
1180, and most of the visible cathedral church
and cloister is a result of numerous building pro-
grammes of the late 12th to early 16th century.

In 1978-80 excavations took place to the east of
the East Cloister in the Camery. Amongst the discoveries was a late Roman mausoleum. There was
also evidence for successive chapels dating from
the Saxon period, and some of the masonry wall
foundations are laid out in the gardens. An exhibi-

Wells Museum.

tion on the archaeology at Wells is located in the Chain Gate at the top of the Chapter House stairs.

To the south of the cathedral is the Bishop's Palace, the gardens of which also open to the public in the summer (for further information contact The Warden, The Palace, Wells. Tel. Wells (0749) 678691).

Reading. Rodwell 1987.

Nearby sites. 58 Ebbor Gorge; 76 Hunter's Lodge Inn; 146 Wells; 158 Wookey Hole.

West Camel Saxon cross.

146 WELLS (Museum)

Location ST 550 459. 8 Cathedral Green, Wells, BA5 2UE. Tel. Wells (0749) 673477. Near the West Front of Wells Cathedral.

Parking. There are several pay car parks in Wells.

Access for disabled visitors. There is access to the ground floor displays, and parking in Cathedral Green.

Facilities. There is a sales area and a toilet in the museum, and banks, shops, toilets and refreshments are available in the town.

Admission charge. A charge is made.

Open. Easter to 30 September: Monday-Saturday 10am-5.30pm, Sundays 11am-5.30pm; October to Easter: Wednesday-Sunday 11am-4pm.

The Museum. There is a variety of collections of important archaeological material from Wells and the surrounding region, including Roman lead ingots from the Mendips, and Iron Age and Roman finds from the Great Cave at Wookey Hole. The

displays are in the process of modernisation.

Nearby sites. 58 Ebbor Gorge; 76 Hunter's Lodge Inn; 145 Wells; 158 Wookey Hole.

147 WEST CAMEL (Saxon cross shaft)

Location ST 580 246. 5.75 kilometres northeast of Ilchester. The cross is in the centre of the north transept of All Saints Church.

Parking. There is parking in the main village street or in the layby by the telephone kiosk, with a very short walk to the church.

Access for disabled visitors. The church is accessible, and there is very limited parking outside the churchyard entrance.

Site description. The fragment of cross shaft was found in 1866 beneath the floor between the nave and chancel. It is made from Bath stone and is 0.75 metres in height. Carving survives on two sides, and a tree scroll and animals with ribbon-like bodies form an interlace design. The cross shaft

Two views of West Luccombe packhorse bridge.

probably dates to the 9th century, and is well
displayed in the church.

A circular Norman font with carved intersecting
arches is situated by the door of the church. On
the wall near the Saxon cross are two carved bench
ends, the remainder having been replaced or lost.

Reading. Foster 1987, 55, 60, 78, fig 3.

Nearby sites. 79 Ilchester; 91 Marston Magna;
100 Nether Adber; 123 South Cadbury Castle.

148 WEST LUCCOMBE (Medieval bridge)

Location SS 898 461. One kilometre south-east
of Porlock. The bridge crosses a stream (Horner
Water) near the junction of the Horner to West
Luccombe road with the road to the Burrowhayes
camping and caravan site. Access is from both
roads.

Parking. There is roadside parking by the east
side of the bridge just south of West Luccombe.

Access for disabled visitors. The bridge is
visible from the road to Burrowhayes.

Site description. The bridge is a narrow single
arched packhorse bridge, only 550 metres to the
north of the Horner packhorse bridge. It is prob-

ably of Medieval construction.

Reading. Jervoise 1930, 113-14.

Nearby sites. 23 Bury Castle; 28 Chapel Cross; 73 Horner; 120 Selworthy.

149 WHITNELL CORNER (Bronze Age round barrows)

Location ST 598 490. 4.5 kilometres north-east of Wells. Three barrows are visible in the pasture field to the north of the Whitnell Corner crossroads (junction of the B3139 and B3135 roads). They are on the crest of a hill 300 metres along the B3139 road, on the west of the road.

Parking. Roadside parking is very limited, and the road is quite busy with traffic.

Access for disabled visitors. The barrows are visible from the road.

Site description. Three prominent Bronze Age round barrows are on the crest of a small hill, two close together and another 100 metres distant. There was originally a much smaller fourth barrow near the road, but this cannot be discerned. Grinsell records the barrows as being covered with oaks and other trees within the Burnt Wood plantation in 1963, but this has since been cleared.

Reading. Grinsell 1971, 106.

Nearby sites. 76, 78 Hunter's Lodge Inn; 88 Maesbury Castle; 150 Whitnell Corner.

150 WHITNELL CORNER (Bronze Age round barrow)

Location ST 596 486. Five kilometres north-east of Wells. This fairly prominent barrow is close to the road in a field to the north-east of Victoria Farm, 550 metres north-east of the Slab House Inn. It is close to the Whitnell Corner crossroads (150 metres to the north-east), which forms the junction of the B3135 and B3139 roads.

Parking. There is very limited roadside parking on the opposite side of the road, but the road is quite busy with traffic.

Access for disabled visitors. The barrow is visible from the roadside.

Site description. This round barrow is 1.5 metres high and is probably of Bronze Age date. It was apparently opened 'for a pot of gold', but only bones were found.

Whit Stones near Porlock.

Reading. Grinsell 1971, 69 (St. Cuthbert Out 23: should be 33), 117 (incorrect grid reference).

Nearby sites. 76, 78 Hunter's Lodge Inn; 88 Maesbury Castle; 149 Whitnell Corner.

151 WHIT STONES, Porlock Common (Bronze Age standing stones)

Location SS 853 462. Three kilometres WSW of Porlock. The stones are about 100 metres south of the A39 road in heather moor. Only a faint path leads to the stones from the car park.

Parking. There is a car park nearly opposite, on the north of the road (the westerly of two car parks along this stretch of the road).

Access for disabled visitors. None and the stones cannot be seen clearly from the road.

Site description. Two large standing stones on Porlock Common both lean 60-70 degrees to the east, and are about 0.9 metres high. Their origin is uncertain, but they may be Bronze Age standing stones or even the remains of a stone circle. They were mentioned in Exmoor Forest perambulations from 1219 when they were known by their present name, although in the perambulations of 1279, 1298 and 1301 'Fifstane' or 'Fifstones' are mentioned. The Rev. John Skinner sketched the stones in 1836. The southernmost stone has an engraved Ordnance Survey bench mark. The Whit Stones are said to have been hurled by the Devil from Hurlestone Point, and to have resulted from a throwing competition between the Devil and a Giant.

Reading. Fowler 1988, 10; Grinsell 1969, 14;

Grinsell 1970, 17 (plate), 48-9.

Nearby sites. 43 Culbone Hill; 73 Horner; 87 Madacombe; 107 Porlock Common.

152 WICK BARROW, Hinkley Point
(Bronze Age round barrow)

Location ST 209 455. Twelve kilometres north-west of Bridgwater, adjacent to Hinkley Point Nuclear Power Station. The barrow lies at the western end of the road from Cannington to Hinkley just within the perimeter fence of the power station, near a Nuclear Electric sign. It is close to the road, covered in scrub and small trees, and is enclosed by a barbed wire fence.

Parking. There is a layby about 200 metres to the south of the barrow on the east of the road, or limited roadside parking.

Access for disabled visitors. The barrow is visible from the roadside.

The site. The round barrow is situated on a slightly elevated outcrop of Lower Lias limestone and overlooks Wick Moor which is likely to have been an inlet of the sea when the barrow was constructed in the early Bronze Age. It used to be in the middle of a field, but the road system has since changed. The barrow was excavated in 1907 and was found to be a cairn of lias blocks about 24.4 metres in diameter and 3.4 metres high. It covered a smaller barrow 9.1 metres in diameter, revetted on the exterior by a substantial drystone wall 1.1 metres high. The central primary burial of the barrow was removed in Roman times, but three contracted secondary Beaker burials were found during the excavations. Each burial was accompanied by a Beaker pot, and two were accompanied by flint implements, one of which was a fine flint dagger. The finds are now on display in the County Museum, Taunton, as well as a model of the barrow.

The site is also known as Burrow Sidwell or Pixies' Mound as pixies were supposed to live in the mound. Various legends are associated with the mound, including that of it shifting its position in the field from time to time. Another legend states that if it is removed by day, it will be replaced during the night, and that harm would come to anyone breaking into the mound.

Reading. Gray 1909 (on the excavations and folklore); Grinsell 1969, 39; Grinsell, 1976a, 104.

Nearby sites. 62 Fiddington; 85 Lilstock; 101 Nether Stowey; 127 Stogursey.

Williton, see **Battlegore, Williton.**
Winsford Hill, see **Caratacus Stone,** and **Wambarrows.**

153 WITCOMBE (Deserted Medieval Village)

Location ST 487 161. One kilometre south-west of Montacute. The earthworks are situated on the south-east of Ham Hill hillfort, on a part called Butcher's Hill. Opposite the junction of the road from Ham Hill to Montacute with the road from Ham Hill to Odcombe (at ST 491 163), a footpath signposted 'Westbury ¾m' leads to the site. Follow the trackway for 230 metres to a junction where there are several field gates. Turn right through the gateway, following the yellow waymark sign. At this point terraces or strip lynchets can be seen on the hillside. Follow the track down into the valley, where the field system can still be seen on the hillside. The irregular earthworks and hollow way of the village are in the bottom of the valley. The footpath then continues into the next field away from the site.

An alternative route is to walk from the priory at Montacute.

Parking. Roadside parking is difficult; easier parking is available at Montacute, but with a longer walk to the site.

Access for disabled visitors. None.

Site description. The visible earthworks represent the deserted hamlet of Witcombe or Widcombe. Half the valley has been ploughed, and in this area the earthworks are quite indistinct, but those in the south-west part of the valley are fairly prominent. The earthworks include hollow ways, small enclosures, house platforms and a pond, and above the settlement on the hillside are strip lynchets representing former cultivation. The hamlet was mentioned in the Domesday book of 1086, and was still in existence by 1566, but by 1614 it was largely deserted. The main hollow way running the length of the valley was once thought to be a Roman road, but it is much more likely to be a Medieval road related to Witcombe.

Nearby sites. 72 Ham Hill; 95, 96, 97 Montacute.

154 WITHAM (Carthusian priory)

Location ST 757 417. Six kilometres SSW of Frome. The priory is bisected by the railway line and is adjacent to the road north-east of Witham Friary village, opposite Witham Hall Farm. The two elements of the site to visit are the fishponds and the earthworks within the precinct boundary. Roadside parking is very limited. There is parking space further east along the road (at ST 760 419) right by the railway opposite a trackway, just west of a row of houses. From there, walk towards Witham Hall Farm. Just beyond the farm on the left (south) of the road, earthworks can be seen in the pasture field from the metal field gate. Opposite a silage clamp is another metal gate for the next field: go through this gateway, and the footpath follows the hedge line (the line of the precinct wall). In this field earthworks are visible, probably relating to the priory or the later house. At the end of the field, cross the stile, and with caution cross the railway tracks and then the next stile. The footpath continues alongside the hedge (also the line of the precinct wall), but the earthworks in the field to the east are difficult to see from the path.

Return to the road. Go past the silage clamp, over the little bridge, and turn left (south) onto the trackway where there is a footpath sign to Witham Friary. The right of way follows the hedge line on the right, and to the left of the path are the Medieval fish ponds. Parking is possible in this field for those fishing in the ponds (day and night tickets available).

Access for disabled visitors. Parking is possible on the road near the fishponds from where they are partly visible, as well as earthworks in the field to the east.

Site description. As part of his penance for the murder of Archbishop Thomas of Canterbury, Henry II founded a house of Carthusians (the most austere monastic order) at Witham around 1179. There were difficulties in establishing the priory until the appointment of Hugh of Avalon (St. Hugh of Lincoln) as prior, but from about 1180-86 he succeeded in constructing the priory buildings. Witham was the first Carthusian foundation in England, and was also known as Witham Charterhouse or Selwood. Not a great deal is known about the history of the priory, although during the Black Death all the lay brothers perished; the

Seal from Witham Priory.

mortality amongst the monks is not known.

The priory was surrendered to the Crown in March 1539, and many buildings were demolished and the church bells and lead roof melted down. The site was purchased by Ralph Hopton for £20, and he built Witham House by converting some of the monastery buildings. In the 18th century this was converted into a stately mansion, but it was hardly ever lived in and seems to have been demolished in the early 19th century. All trace of the priory and house disappeared and the site was forgotten, until earlier this century when the Dean of Wells discovered, in the chapter library, the original foundation charter, granted by Henry II and dating to January 1182. The earthworks that are now visible relate to both the mansion and its garden and to the Carthusian priory. The hedge boundaries of the field opposite the farm and the field to the south (on the other side of the railway) form a rectangle and represent the line of the original priory precinct wall. Excavations took place in 1921 and during the 1960s, and have proved the identification of the priory site. Several large fishponds belonging to the priory are still used by anglers today.

Witham Friary is often confused with the site of the priory but actually refers to the nearby village in which the lay brothers' church was situated.

Reading. Aston & Dennison 1988, 395, fig. 5; Colt Hoare 1824, 5-39; McGarvie 1981; Robinson 1918; Scott Holmes 1911, 123-8; Thompson 1895.

Nearby sites. 90 Marston; 92 Marston Moat; 103 Nunney Castle; 155 Witham Friary.

155 WITHAM FRIARY (Monastic chapel and dovecote)

Location ST 743 411. Seven kilometres south-west of Frome. The church is in the centre of the village next to Manor Farm. The dovecote is opposite Manor Farm to the rear of the recreation field at the top of a small lane with houses.

Parking. There is room to park near the church or by the recreation field.

Access for disabled visitors. The church and dovecote can be viewed from the exterior, and adjacent parking is possible.

Site description. Witham Friary was the name given to the village occupied by the lay brothers of the nearby Witham priory and means literally 'Witham of the lay brothers (fratres)'. The lay chapel had probably been previously built by Bruton priory, but it then passed to Witham Priory and was refurbished by St. Hugh of Lincoln in the late 12th century. This refurbishment included the construction of the stone vaulted roof, a very unusual feature for an English parish church. On the dissolution of Witham Priory in 1539, the lay brothers' chapel continued in use as the parish church. The massive flying buttresses, built in 1875 to strengthen the church, were copied from St. Hugh's Cathedral in Lincoln.

The Friary Grange was situated next to the church, and opposite the church was the dovecote, also part of the Friary Grange. The dovecote is still standing and is unusual in being a rectangular structure with massive walls and buttresses at the corners. It is of late 14th century date and was restored in the early 20th century.

Reading. McGarvie 1981; Thompson 1895.

Nearby sites. 90 Marston; 92 Marston Moat; 103 Nunney Castle; 154 Witham.

156 WITHYPOOL (Bronze Age stone circle)

Location and parking SS 837 343.
9.5 kilometres north-west of Dulverton. The circle is on the south-west side of Withypool Hill. A footpath passes across the moor fairly close to the monument, but there is no right of way across the monument. There is roadside parking near the cattle grid on Two Moors Way (SS 846 338). From here walk westwards for nearly one kilometre. The footpath can also be joined from the South Molton road to the west, but parking is difficult. Right on top of Withypool Hill is a barrow at SS 840 344. There is no right of way to the barrow.

Access for disabled visitors. None.

Site description. This rare example of a Bronze Age stone circle in Somerset is unfortunately very insubstantial and partly hidden in heather. There were originally thirty-seven small stones recorded (when the circle was built, there were probably about one hundred), but there are now only twenty-seven standing, with another three recumbent. None is more than 0.6 metres high and most are 0.1 metres high. The circle is almost thirty-seven metres in diameter. The site was discovered in 1898, and a plan of the thirty-seven stones was later drawn and each one recorded by Gray.

On top of Withypool Hill is a large squashed-looking round barrow which measures 18.3 metres across and 0.9 metres high and has been mutilated.

Reading. Fowler 1988, 11; Gray 1907.

Nearby sites. 24 Caratacus Stone; 41 Cow Castle; 71 Green Barrow and Brightworthy Barrows; 132 Tarr Steps.

Wittenham, see **Rowley**.

157 WIVELISCOMBE BARROW (Bronze Age round barrow)

Location and parking ST 005 348.
Ten kilometres north-west of Wiveliscombe. The barrow is in the north-east corner of a pasture field near the south side of the Brendon Hill to Wheddon Cross road. It can be viewed from a nearby metal field gate, but parking is difficult.

Access for disabled visitors. None.

Site description. This Bronze Age round barrow has in the past also been called 'Eastern Barrow'.

Reading. Grinsell 1969, 16, 28.

Nearby sites. 37 Clatworthy Camp; 75 Huish Champflower Barrow; 114, 115 Ralegh's Cross.

158 WOOKEY HOLE CAVES (Caves with Palaeolithic and later occupation; museum)

Location ST 532 479. 2.5 kilometres north-west of Wells. The site is not in the village of Wookey, but is reached from a minor road (Haybridge to Wookey Hole) leading northwards from the A371

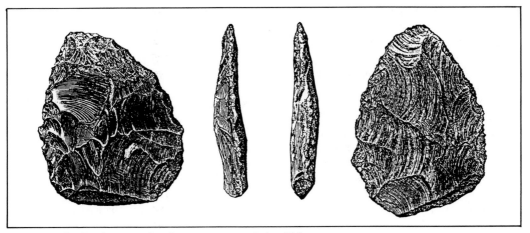

Palaeolithic flint handaxes found in the Hyaena Den, Wookey Hole.

road. It is well signposted. Wookey Hole Caves, Wells, Somerset, BA5 1BB. Tel. Wells (0749) 672243.

Parking. A large car park is on the west of the road at Wookey Hole Caves and Mill (at ST 531 476).

Access for disabled visitors. None (except for the mill).

Facilities. There are toilets in the car park and in the paper mill, a cafeteria at the car park, and a shop in the paper mill and another by the car park, and refreshments in the village.

Admission charge. A charge is made.

Open. Every day (except the week before Christmas), 9.30am-5.30pm (last admission) summer, 10.30am-4.30pm winter.

Site description. Wookey Hole is now a highly commercialised tourist attraction. The limestone Mendips contain numerous caves, and the Wookey Hole caves lie in a ravine cut by the River Axe. Modern diving has revealed many new chambers. The river issues from a lower cave mouth, above which is a narrow higher entrance (now used by visitors), leading into the Great Cave (show cave). The mouth of this cave was occupied intermittently during the Iron Age and Roman period, resulting in over a metre of stratified deposits, including many animal and human remains.

The caves occupied by early man are not readily accessible, although a pathway from the show caves passes the Hyaena Den (ST 531 480) which

was almost completely excavated between 1859 and 1874 and reinvestigated between 1966 and 1970. As well as being used by wild animals, these caves were also used by man during the Middle and Upper Palaeolithic (from around 35,000 BC), for which the evidence includes finds of hearths and stone tools. High above the Hyaena Den is the Badger Hole at about ten metres above the floor of the ravine. This cave was investigated from 1938, and was found to have been occupied by man during the Upper Palaeolithic. In the cave were tools of flint (such as handaxes), as well as many animal bones. Several of the caves were also used in later archaeological periods. Many finds from the Wookey Hole caves are in Wells Museum, and in the site museum.

A paper mill is part of the visitor attractions, and a mill has existed at Wookey Hole since at least the 11th century. By 1610 it was used as a paper mill and a paper mill has been in production here until the 20th century; in 1976 the industry was revived.

Reading. Balch 1914; Campbell 1977, 49-51, 99, 100-1, 113, maps 10, 36, figs 10, 11; Cook 1982; Hawkes et al 1978; Tratman et al 1971.

Nearby sites. 57, 58 Ebbor; 109 Priddy; 116 Ramspits.

159 WRIGHT'S PIECE (Bronze Age round barrows)

Location ST 531 547. 6.75 kilometres ENE of Cheddar. The barrows are on the north-east side of the B3134 road in an area once known as Wright's Piece, 750 metres south-east of the B3134 and B3371 crossroads. Cross the stile by the road and follow the footpath for 100 metres alongside the drystone wall field boundary. On the other side of the wall is a low mutilated round barrow. In the same field as the footpath, three other low round barrows can be seen, one of which is on the other side (north-west) of a modern fence.

Parking. There is very limited roadside parking.

Access for disabled visitors. The barrows can be seen from the road.

Site description. These four round barrows are in a line, and are situated in an area of the Mendips where there are numerous Bronze Age barrows. On the opposite side of the road, about 300 metres distant, there is another group of five barrows at ST 527 545; they are just visible from the footpath leading south-westwards to Haydon Grange. These two groups of barrows have been considered to be a single cemetery, and have sometimes been named collectively 'the Nordrach barrows', although Nordrach is nearly two kilometres to the north-west.

Reading. Burrow 1924, 22 (with figure); Grinsell 1971, 102, 122; Thomas 1976, 189.

Nearby sites. 3 Ashen Hill Barrows; 86 Lord's Lot; 111 Priddy Circles; 113 Priddy.

160 YEOVIL, The Museum of South Somerset

Location ST 554 157. Adjacent to the large car park by the Octagon Theatre off the street called Hendford. Museum of South Somerset, Hendford, BA20 1UN. Tel. Yeovil (0935) 24774.

Parking. There is parking in the adjacent Petters Way pay car park.

Access for disabled visitors. There is access to the exhibition area downstairs but not to the archaeology displays or toilets. Parking is sometimes available outside the museum.

Facilities. There is a sales area and toilets. Refreshments, shops and banks are available in the town.

Open. Tuesday to Saturday 10am-4pm, Sunday 2-6pm. Open Bank Holiday Mondays. Other Mondays, parties only, by appointment.

The Museum. The museum has been extensively refurbished, and was re-opened in 1991. It is run by South Somerset District Council in a building that was once the coach house of the Manor House. The Hayward Gallery upstairs houses the archaeology displays which include a model of South Cadbury hillfort, Bronze Age axes, and an extensive display on the Roman period with various artefacts, a reconstruction of a dining room on an original mosaic floor from the nearby Lufton villa, a life-size reconstruction of a kitchen, a display of pottery, and models of villas.

Nearby sites. 21 Brympton House; 95, 96, 97 Montacute.

Additional Information

Sites by Period

See also list of museums under Main Types of Site, as individual museums contain displays representing a range of periods of time.

Palaeolithic

35   Cheddar Gorge (caves)
58   Ebbor Gorge (caves)
158   Wookey Hole Caves

Mesolithic

35   Cheddar Gorge (caves)

Neolithic

7   Battlegore, Williton (long barrow)
9   Beacon Batch, Black Down (long barrow)
58   Ebbor Gorge (caves)
76   Hunter's Lodge Inn (henge)
111   Priddy Circles (henges)

Bronze Age

1   Alderman's Barrow
3   Ashen Hill Barrows, Priddy
7   Battlegore, Williton (barrows)
9   Beacon Batch, Black Down (barrows)
10   Beacon Hill, near Shepton Mallet (barrows)
13   Black Down (barrows)
15   Blue Gate, Exmoor (barrow)
16   Brean Down (barrows)
40   County Gate (barrows)
49   Dunkery Beacon (barrows)
57   Ebbor: Deer Leap Stones (standing stones)
58   Ebbor Gorge (caves)
70   Great Rowbarrow and Little Rowbarrow (barrows)
71   Green Barrow and Brightworthy Barrows
75   Huish Champflower Barrow
76   Hunter's Lodge Inn (barrow)

77   Hunter's Lodge Inn (barrow)
78   Hunter's Lodge Inn (barrow)
81   Joaney How and Robin How (barrows)
86   Lord's Lot (barrow)
87   Madacombe (barrows)
102   Norton Fitzwarren (enclosure)
107   Porlock Common (stone circle, barrow)
108   Priddy (barrow)
109   Priddy (barrow)
110   Priddy (barrows)
111   Priddy Circles (henges)
112   Priddy Nine Barrows
113   Priddy Nine Barrows Lane (barrow)
115   Ralegh's Cross (barrow)
117   Robin Hood's Butts (barrows)
118   Rowberrow (barrow)
121   Selworthy Beacon (barrows)
138   Two Barrows
139   Tyning's Farm (barrows)
141   Wambarrows, Winsford Hill (barrows)
149   Whitnell Corner (barrows)
150   Whitnell Corner (barrow)
151   Whit Stones, Porlock Common (standing stones)
152   Wick Barrow, Hinkley Point
157   Wiveliscombe Barrow
159   Wright's Piece (barrows)

Iron Age

8   Bat's Castle (hillfort)
12   Black Ball Camp (hillfort)
14   Blacker's Hill, Chilcompton (hillfort)
16   Brean Down (hillfort, field systems)
17   Brent Knoll (hillfort)
23   Bury Castle, Selworthy (hillfort)
27   Castle Neroche (earthworks)
37   Clatworthy Camp (hillfort)
41   Cow Castle (hillfort)

45   Dead Woman's Ditch (linear earthwork)
47   Dowsborough (hillfort)
58   Ebbor Gorge (caves)
59   Elworthy Barrows (hillfort)
64   Gallox Hill (linear earthwork)
68   Glastonbury (lake village)
72   Ham Hill (hillfort)
82   Kenwalch's Castle (hillfort)
84   Kingsdown Camp (hillfort)
88   Maesbury Castle (hillfort)
94   Meare Lake Villages
102 Norton Fitzwarren (hillfort)
105 Plainsfield Camp (hillfort)
106 Ponter's Ball Dyke (linear earthwork)
122 Small Down Camp (hillfort)
123 South Cadbury Castle (hillfort)
131 Sweetworthy (hillfort)
137 Trendle Ring (hillfort)
158 Wookey Hole Caves

Roman

17   Brent Knoll (hillfort)
21   Brympton House, Brympton D'Evercy (mosaic)
30   Charterhouse-on-Mendip (lead mining site, fort)
31   Charterhouse-on-Mendip (amphitheatre)
58   Ebbor Gorge (caves)
79   Ilchester (town)
84   Kingsdown Camp (hillfort)
102 Norton Fitzwarren (hillfort)
158 Wookey Hole Caves

Dark Ages/ Saxon

2   Aller (font)
4   Athelney Abbey
24   Caratacus Stone, Winsford Hill
27   Castle Neroche (earthwork)
34   Cheddar (palace)
43   Culbone Hill (inscribed stone)
44   Daw's Castle, Watchet (burh)
65   Glastonbury (abbey)
69   Glastonbury Tor (Dark Age occupation)
89   Maperton (sculptured stone)
98   Muchelney (monastery)
123 South Cadbury Castle (hillfort)
145 Wells Cathedral
147 West Camel (cross)

Medieval

4   Athelney Abbey
6   Ballands Castle, Penselwood
11   Bishops Lydeard (crosses)
18   Bridgwater (castle)
20   Bruton (priory wall)
22   Burrow Mump, Burrowbridge (church ruins)
25   Cart Gate, near Martock (ridge-and-furrow)
26   Castle Cary (castle)
27   Castle Neroche (castle)
28   Chapel Cross: St. Andrew's Chapel
32   Charterhouse-on-Mendip (enclosure)
33   Charterhouse-on-Mendip (enclosure)
34   Cheddar (chapel, palace)
36   Clanville (ridge-and-furrow)
38   Cleeve Abbey, Washford
39   Coat (ridge-and-furrow)
42   Crowcombe (crosses, church house)
46   Downend (castle)
47   Drayton (cross)
50   Dunster (castle)
51   Dunster: Butter Cross
52   Dunster (priory)
53   Dunster: Gallox Bridge
55   East Lydford (church ruins)
60   Farleigh Hungerford (castle)
61   Fenny Castle
62   Fiddington (sheila-na-gig, cross)
65   Glastonbury (abbey)
66   Glastonbury (priory barn)
69   Glastonbury (Tribunal)
69   Glastonbury (Tor)
73   Horner (bridge)
74   Horsington (cross)
79   Ilchester (town)
83   Kilve (chantry ruins)
85   Lilstock: St. Andrew's Church
90   Marston (deserted Medieval village)
91   Marston Magna (moated site, ridge-and-furrow)
92   Marston Moat
93   Meare Fish House
95   Montacute (cross)
96   Montacute (priory)
97   Montacute: St. Michael's Hill (castle)
98   Muchelney (priory)
99   Muchelney (cross)
100 Nether Adber ((deserted Medieval village)

101	Nether Stowey (castle)	123	South Cadbury Castle
103	Nunney Castle	131	Sweetworthy
114	Ralegh's Cross	137	Trendle Ring
116	Ramspits, Deer Leap (deserted farmstead, field system)		

101   Nether Stowey (castle)
103   Nunney Castle
114   Ralegh's Cross
116   Ramspits, Deer Leap (deserted farmstead, field system)
119   Rowley (deserted Medieval village)
120   Selworthy (cross)
124   Spargrove (moated site)
125   Spaxton (cross)
126   Stavordale Priory
127   Stogursey (castle, cross, well)
128   Stoke-sub-Hamdon (chantry)
129   Stowell (deserted Medieval village)
132   Tarr Steps (bridge)
134   Taunton (castle)
135   Taunton (priory barn)
136   Taunton: St. Margaret's Leper Hospital
140   Upton: St. James' Church
143   Wedmore (cross)
144   Wedmore (cross)
145   Wells Cathedral
148   West Luccombe (bridge)
153   Witcombe (deserted Medieval village)
154   Witham (priory)
155   Witham Friary (monastic chapel, dovecote)

Main Types of Site

Hillforts/ enclosures

8   Bat's Castle
12   Black Ball Camp
14   Blacker's Hill, Chilcompton
16   Brean Down
17   Brent Knoll
23   Bury Castle, Selworthy
27   Castle Neroche
37   Clatworthy Camp
41   Cow Castle
47   Dowsborough
59   Elworthy Barrows
72   Hám Hill
82   Kenwalch's Castle
84   Kingsdown Camp
88   Maesbury Castle
102   Norton Fitzwarren
105   Plainsfield Camp
122   Small Down Camp

123   South Cadbury Castle
131   Sweetworthy
137   Trendle Ring

Round Barrows

1   Alderman's Barrow
3   Ashen Hill Barrows, Priddy
7   Battlegore, Williton
9   Beacon Batch, Black Down
13   Black Down
15   Blue Gate, Exmoor
16   Brean Down
40   County Gate
49   Dunkery Beacon
70   Great Rowbarrow and Little Rowbarrow
71   Green Barrow and Brightworthy Barrows
75   Huish Champflower Barrow
76   Hunter's Lodge Inn
77   Hunter's Lodge Inn
78   Hunter's Lodge Inn
81   Joaney How and Robin How
86   Lord's Lot
87   Madacombe
107   Porlock Common
108   Priddy
109   Priddy
110   Priddy
112   Priddy Nine Barrows
113   Priddy: Nine Barrows Lane
115   Ralegh's Cross
117   Robin Hood's Butt
118   Rowberrow
121   Selworthy Beacon
138   Two Barrows
139   Tyning's Farm
141   Wambarrows, Winsford Hill
149   Whitnell Corner
150   Whitnell Corner
152   Wick Barrow, Hinkley Point
157   Wiveliscombe Barrow
159   Wright's Piece

Long Barrows

7   Battlegore, Williton
9   Beacon Batch, Black Down

Moated Sites

91 Marston Magna
92 Marston Moat
124 Spargrove

Church/ Chapel Ruins

22 Burrow Mump, Burrowbridge
28 Chapel Cross: St. Andrew's Chapel
34 Cheddar
56 East Lydford
69 Glastonbury Tor
85 Lilstock: St. Andrew's Church
140 Upton: St. James' Church
145 Wells Cathedral

Museums/Exhibitions

5 Axbridge: King John's Hunting Lodge
19 Bridgwater: Admiral Blake Museum
29 Chard Museum
35 Cheddar Gorge
54 Dunster: Visitor Centre
63 Frome Museum
65 Glastonbury (priory)
66 Glastonbury (priory barn)
67 Glastonbury (Tribunal)
80 Ilchester
104 Peat Moors Visitor Centre
130 Street (Shoe Museum)
133 Taunton (County Museum)
135 Taunton (Priory Barn)
142 Watchet: Market House Museum
145 Wells Cathedral
146 Wells Museum
158 Wookey Hole Caves
160 Yeovil: The Museum of South Somerset

Sites to Visit in Wet Weather

Sites under Shelter

2 Aller (Saxon font; King Alfred's window)
5 Axbridge: King John's Hunting Lodge (museum)
19 Bridgwater: Admiral Blake Museum
21 Brympton House, Brympton D'Evercy (Roman mosaic)
29 Chard Museum
35 Cheddar Gorge (caves, museum)
54 Dunster Visitor Centre
63 Frome Museum
66 Glastonbury (priory barn)
67 Glastonbury (Tribunal)
80 Ilchester (museum)
89 Maperton (Saxon sculptured stone)
104 Peat Moors Visitors Centre
130 Street (The Shoe Museum)
133 Taunton (County Museum)
135 Taunton (Priory Barn)
142 Watchet: Market House Museum
146 Wells Museum
147 West Camel (Saxon cross shaft)
155 Witham (monastic chapel)
158 Wookey Hole Caves
160 Yeovil: The Museum of South Somerset

Sites Partly under Shelter

38 Cleeve Abbey, Washford
50 Dunster (castle)
52 Dunster (priory)
60 Farleigh Hungerford (castle)
65 Glastonbury Abbey
85 Lilstock: St. Andrew's Church
93 Meare Fish House
98 Muchelney (priory)
128 Stoke-sub-Hamdon (chantry)
134 Taunton (castle)
140 Upton: St. James' Church
145 Wells Cathedral

Rights of Way

The following authorities should be contacted over problems with rights of way, including obstructions such as ploughed paths, barbed wire and bulls.

Exmoor National Park: Head Ranger, Exmoor National Park Authority, Exmoor House, Dulverton, TA22 9HL.

Mendip District: obstructions on footpaths in this district are dealt with by Somerset County Council, Environment Department, The Group Manager, Rights of Way, County Hall, Taunton, TA1 3DY. Tel. Taunton (0823) 255624.

Sedgemoor District: Environmental Services, Sedgemoor District Council, Bridgwater House, King's Square, Bridgwater, TA6 3AR. Tel. Bridgwater (0278) 424391.

South Somerset District: Rights of Way Officer, Leisure & Arts Department, South Somerset District Council, PO Box 33, The Council Offices, Brympton Way, Yeovil, BA20 1PU. Tel. Yeovil (0935) 75272.

Taunton Deane: Secretarial and Legal Division, Taunton Deane Borough Council, The Deane House, Belvedere Road, Taunton, TA1 1HE. Tel. Taunton (0823) 335166 ext. 2306.

West Somerset District: the area outside the Exmoor National Park is dealt with by West Somerset District Council, Technical Offices, 20 Fore Street, Williton, TA4 4QA. Tel. Williton (0984) 32291.

Bibliography and Further Reading

ABBREVIATIONS

BAR   British Archaeological Report
Proc.SANHS Proceedings of the Somerset Archaeological and Natural History Society
Proc.UBSS   Proceedings of the University of Bristol Spelaeological Society

Abrams, L. & Carley, J.P. (eds) 1991 *The Archaeology and History of Glastonbury Abbey. Essays in Honour of the Ninetieth Birthday of C.A. Ralegh Radford* (The Boydell Press, Woodbridge).

Adkins, L. & Adkins, R. 1982 *The Handbook of British Archaeology* (Papermac, London).

Adkins, L. & Adkins, R. 1989a *An Introduction to Archaeology* (The Apple Press, London).

Adkins, L & Adkins, R.A. 1989b Excavation on St. Michael's Hill, Montacute *Proc.SANHS* 133, 125-9.

Alcock, L. 1972 *'By South Cadbury, is that Camelot...'. Excavations at Cadbury Castle 1966-70* (Thames & Hudson, London).

Allcroft, A.H. 1908 *Earthwork of England, Prehistoric, Roman, Saxon, Danish, Norman and Medieval* (Macmillan, London).

Andrews, P. 1990 *Owls, caves and fossils. Predation, preservation and accumulation of small mammal bones in caves, with an analysis of the Pleistocene cave faunas from Westbury-sub-Mendip, Somerset, UK* (Natural History Museum Publications, London).

Ashe, G. (ed) 1968 *The Quest for Arthur's Britain* (London).

Aston, M. 1977 Deserted settlements in Mudford parish, Yeovil *Proc.SANHS* 121, 41-53.

Aston, M. 1979 A Sheila-na-gig at Fiddington *Proc.SANHS* 123, 111-13.

Aston, M. 1982 The Medieval pattern 1000-1500 AD, pp. 123-33 in Aston & Burrow (eds) 1982.

Aston, M. 1983 Deserted farmsteads on Exmoor and the Lay Subsidy of 1327 in West Somerset *Proc.SANHS* 127, 71-104.

Aston, M. 1984 The towns of Somerset, pp. 167-201 in Haslam (ed) 1984.

Aston, M. 1988a Settlement patterns and forms, pp. 67-81 in Aston (ed) 1988.

Aston, M. 1988b Land use and field systems, pp. 83-97 in Aston (ed) 1988a.

Aston, M. (ed) 1988a *Aspects of the Medieval Landscape of Somerset and Contributions to the Landscape* (Somerset County Council).

Aston, M. (ed) 1988b *Medieval fish, fisheries and fishponds in England* (BAR 182).

Aston, M. (ed) 1989 *Rural Settlements of Medieval England* (Blackwell).

Aston, M. & Burrow, I. 1982 The early Christian centres 600-1000 AD, pp. 119-21 in Aston & Burrow (eds) 1982.

Aston, M. & Burrow, I. (eds) 1982 *The Archaeology of Somerset. A review to 1500 AD* (Somerset County Council).

Aston, M. & Dennison, E. 1988 Fishponds in

Somerset, pp. 391-407 in Aston, M. (ed) 1988b.

Aston, M. & Dennison, E. 1989 A regional study of deserted settlements in the West of England, pp.105-28 in Aston (ed) 1989.

Aston, M. & Leech, R. 1977 *Historic Towns in Somerset. Archaeology and planning* (Bristol).

Aston, M.A. & Murless, B.J. 1978 Somerset archaeology 1977 *Proc.SANHS* 122, 117-52.

Balch, H.E. 1914 *Wookey Hole. Its caves and cave-dwellers* (Oxford University Press).

Barrington, N. & Stanton, W. 1976 *Mendip. The complete caves and a view of the hills* (Bardon Productions, Cheddar).

Bascombe, K.N. 1989 Documentary, pp. 478-83 in Huggins 1989.

Bates, E.H. 1888 Leland in Somersetshire, 1540-1542 *Proc. SANHS* 33, 60-136.

Bates, E.H. 1905 Stavordale Priory *Proc. SANHS* 50, 94-103.

Bell, M. 1990 *Brean Down Excavations 1983-1987* (English Heritage).

Bettey, J. 1988 The church in the landscape. Part 2 from the Norman Conquest to the Reformation, pp. 55-65 in Aston (ed) 1988a.

Bishop, M.J. 1975 Earliest record of man's presence in Britain *Nature* 253, 95-7.

Bond, J. 1988 Glastonbury Abbey barn: the southeast porch *Proc.SANHS* 132, 251-6.

Bond. C.J. & Weller. J.B. 1991 The Somerset Barns of Glastonbury Abbey, pp. 57-87 in Abrams & Carley (eds) 1991.

Bothamley, C.H. 1911 Ancient earthworks, pp. 467-532 in Page (ed) 1911.

Bridge, M. & Dunning, R.W. 1981 The abbey barn *Proc.SANHS* 125, 120.

Brown, K., Croft, R. & Lillford, R. 1988 Conserving the historic landscape, pp. 109-27 in Aston (ed) 1988a.

Bryant, T.C. 1984 Caratacus Stone – a new interpretation *Proc.SANHS* 128, 32-3.

Budge, A.R., Russell, J.R., & Boon, G.C. 1974 Excavations and fieldwork at Charterhouse-on-Mendip, 1960-67 *Proc.UBSS* 13 (13), 327-47.

Bulleid, A. 1893 Ancient canoe found near Glastonbury *Somerset & Dorset Notes & Queries* 3, 121, pl. XX.

Bulleid, A. & Gray, H. St. G. 1911 *The Glastonbury Lake Village. A full description of the excavations and the relics discovered, 1892-1907* Volumes 1 &

2 (Glastonbury Antiquarian Society).

Burnham, B.C. & Wacher, J. 1990 *The 'Small Towns' of Roman Britain* (Batsford, London).

Burrow, E.J. 1924 *Ancient Earthworks & Camps of Somerset* (Cheltenham).

Burrow, I. 1981 *Hillfort and hill-top settlement in Somerset in the first to eighth centuries A.D.* (BAR 91).

Burrow, I. 1982 Hillforts and hilltops 1000 BC-1000 AD, pp. 83-97 in Aston & Burrow (eds) 1982.

Burrow, I. 1984 Excavations at Mill Lane, 1980 – the castle moat and associated features, pp. 53-8 in Leach (ed) 1984.

Bush, R.J.E. 1974 East Lydford, pp.120-9 in Dunning (ed) 1974.

Bush, R.J.E. 1984 The priory of St. Peter and St. Paul, pp. 104-6 in Leach (ed) 1984.

Bush, R.J.E. 1985 Crowcombe, pp. 54-64 in Dunning (ed) 1985.

Bush, R. 1988 *Taunton Castle. A pictorial history* (Somerset Archaeological & Natural History Society).

Bush, R.J.E. & Meek, M. 1984 The castle: history and documentation, pp. 11-16 in Leach (ed) 1984.

Byford, E. 1987 *Somerset Curiosities* (The Dovecote Press).

Campbell, J.B. 1977 *The Upper Palaeolithic of Britain. A study of man and nature in the Late Ice Age* (Oxford University Press).

Carley, J.P. 1988 *Glastonbury Abbey. The Holy House at the head of the Moors Adventurous* (The Boydell Press).

Chadwyck Healey, C.E.H. 1901 *The History of the Part of West Somerset* (London).

Chater, A.G. & Major, A.F. 1910 Excavations at Downend, near Bridgwater, 1908 *Proc.SANHS* 55, 162-74.

Clark, J. 1855 *The Avalonian Guide to the Town of Glastonbury and its Environs* (Bridgwater).

Clements, C.F. 1984 The inner ward and outer bailey; burials and structures exposed in the 1970s, pp. 26-36 in Leach (ed) 1984.

Coles, B. & J. 1986 *Sweet Track to Glastonbury. The Somerset Levels in prehistory* (Thames & Hudson, London).

Coles, B. & J. 1989 *People of the Wetlands. Bogs, bodies and lake-dwellers* (Thames & Hudson, London).

Coles, J. 1982 Prehistory in the Somerset Levels 4000-100 BC, pp. 29-41 in Aston & Burrow (eds) 1982.

Coles, J.M. 1987 *Meare Village East. The excavations of A. Bulleid and H. St. George Gray 1932-1956* (Somerset Levels Papers 13).

Colt Hoare, R. 1824 *Monastic Remains of the Religious Houses at Witham, Bruton & Stavordale, Somerset* (Frome).

Cook, J. 1982 Traces of early man 600,000-50,000 BC, pp. 5-9 in Aston & Burrow (eds) 1982.

Costen, M. 1988a The late Saxon landscape. The evidence from charters and placenames, pp. 33-47 in Aston (ed) 1988a.

Costen, M. 1988b The church in the landscape. Part I The Anglo- Saxon period, pp. 49-53 in Aston (ed) 1988a.

Cunliffe, B. 1982 Iron Age settlement and pottery 650 BC-60 AD, pp. 53-61 in Aston & Burrow (eds) 1982.

Davison, B.K. 1972 Castle Neroche: an abandoned Norman fortress in South Somerset *Proc.SANHS* 116, 16-58.

de Maré, E. 1954 *The Bridges of Britain* (Batsford, London).

Dobson, D.P. 1931 *The Archaeology of Somerset* (Methuen, London).

Dunning, R.W. 1974a 'Ilchester' pp.179-203 in Dunning (ed) 1974.

Dunning, R.W. 1974b Montacute, pp. 210-24 in Dunning (ed) 1974.

Dunning, R.W. 1985a Kilve pp.96-103 in Dunning (ed) 1985.

Dunning, R.W. 1985b Lilstock pp.103-7 in Dunning (ed) 1985.

Dunning.R.W. 1991 The Tribunal, Glastonbury, Somerset pp. 89-92, in Abrams & Carley (eds) 1991.

Dunning, R.W. (ed) 1974 *A History of the County of Somerset*. Volume III (Oxford University Press).

Dunning, R.W. (ed) 1978 *A History of the County of Somerset*. Volume IV (Oxford University Press).

Dunning, R.W. (ed) 1985 *A History of the County of Somerset*. Volume V (Oxford University Press).

Eardley-Wilmot, H. 1983 *Ancient Exmoor* (The Exmoor Press).

Ellis, P. 1989 Norton Fitzwarren hillfort: a report on the excavations by Nancy and Philip Langmaid between 1968 and 1971 *Proc.SANHS* 133, 1-74.

Ellison, A. 1982 Bronze Age societies 2000-650 BC, pp. 43-51 in Aston & Burrow (eds) 1982.

Ellison, A. 1983 *Medieval villages in south-east Somerset. A survey of the archaeological implications of development within 93 surviving Medieval villages in south-east Somerset (Yeovil district)* (Western Archaeological Trust Survey no 6).

Foster, S. 1987 A gazetteer of the Anglo-Saxon sculpture in historic Somerset *Proc.SANHS* 131, 49-80.

Fowler, M.J.F. 1988 The standing stones of Exmoor: a provisional catalogue of 62 West Somerset sites *Proc.SANHS* 132, 1-13.

Fox, C.H. 1875 *Memorials Descriptive and Historical of Taunton Castle* (Taunton).

Gibb, J.H.P. 1981 The Medieval castle at Dunster *Proc.SANHS* 125, 1-15.

Gilyard-Beer, R. 1960 *Cleeve Abbey, Somerset* (HMSO, London: guidebook).

Gray, H. St. G. 1903 Huish Champflower barrow, near Raleigh's Cross, on the Brendon Hills *Somerset & Dorset Notes & Queries* 8, 303-5.

Gray, H. St. G. 1904 Excavations at Castle Neroche, Somerset, June-July, 1903 *Proc.SANHS* 49, 23-53.

Gray, H. St. G. 1905 Excavations at Small Down Camp, near Evercreech, 1904 *Proc.SANHS* 50, 32-49.

Gray, H. St. G. 1907 The stone circle on Withypool Hill *Proc.SANHS* 52, 42-50.

Gray, H. St. G. 1908 Maesbury Camp, or Masbury Castle *Proc.SANHS* 53, 73-81.

Gray, H. St. G. 1909 Report on the Wick Barrow excavations *Proc.SANHS* 54, 1-78.

Gray, H. St. G. 1910 Excavations at the 'Amphitheatre', Charterhouse-on-Mendip, 1909 *Proc.SANHS* 55, 118-37.

Gray, H. St. G. 1929 The Porlock stone circle, Exmoor *Proc.SANHS* 74, 71-7.

Gray, H. St. G. 1932 Battlegore, Williton *Proc.SANHS* 77, 7-36.

Gray, H. St. G. 1940 Excavations at Burrow Mump, Somerset, 1939 *Proc.SANHS* 85, 95-133.

Grinsell, L.V. 1969 Somerset barrows. Part I: west and south *Proc.SANHS* 113, appendix 1-43.

Grinsell, L.V. 1970 *The Archaeology of Exmoor* (David & Charles, Newton Abbot).

Grinsell, L.V. 1971 Somerset barrows. Part II: north and east *Proc.SANHS* 115, 44-132.

Grinsell, L.V. 1976a *Folklore of Prehistoric Sites in Britain* (David & Charles, Newton Abbot).

Grinsell, L. 1976b *Prehistoric Sites in the Quantock Country* (Somerset Archaeological & Natural History Society).

Grinsell, L.V. 1982 Priddy Nine Barrows: a 'correction' corrected *Proc.SANHS* 126, 103-4.

Harvey, J. 1988 Parks, gardens and landscaping, pp. 99-107 in Aston (ed) 1988a.

Haslam, J. (ed) 1984 *Anglo-Saxon Towns in Southern England* (Phillimore, Chichester).

Haverfield, F.J. 1911 Romano-British Somerset, pp.207-371 in Page (ed) 1911.

Hawkes, C.J., Rogers, J.M. & Tratman, E.K. 1978 Romano-British cemetery in the fourth chamber of Wookey Hole Cave, Somerset *Proc.UBSS* 15 (1), 23-52.

Hershon, C.P. 1990 *The Castles of Cary* (Pavalas Press, Bristol).

Hill, D. 1982 The Anglo-Saxons 700-1066 AD, pp. 109-17 in Aston & Burrow (eds) 1982.

Hinchliffe, J. 1984 Excavations at Canon Street 1977, pp.106-11 in Leach (ed) 1984.

Huggins, P.J. 1989 Excavations of the collegiate and Augustinian churches, *Waltham Abbey Essex Archaeological Journal* 146, 476-537.

Hugo, T. 1859 Muchelney Abbey *Proc.SANHS* 8, 76-132.

Hugo, T. 1860 Taunton Priory *Proc.SANHS* 9, 1-127.

Hugo, T. 1874 *The History of the Hospital of S.Margaret, Taunton* (London).

Hugo, T. 1897 Athelney Abbey *Proc.SANHS* 43, 94-165.

Hunt, T.J. & Sellman, R.R. 1973 *Aspects of Somerset History* (Somerset County Council).

Hurley, J. 1982 (4th ed) *Murder and Mystery on Exmoor* (The Exmoor Press).

Jacobi, R. 1982a Ice Age cave-dwellers 12,000-9,000 BC, pp. 11- 13 in Aston & Burrow (eds) 1982.

Jacobi, R.M. 1982b The environment of man at Cheddar: 11-10,000 years ago *Proc.SANHS* 126, 1-16.

Jervoise, E. 1930 *The Ancient Bridges of the South of England* (The Architectural Press, London).

Knight, C. (ed) 1845 *Old England: A pictorial museum of regal, ecclesiastical, municipal, baronial and popular antiquities volume 1* (London, James Sangster and Co.).

Leach, P.J. 1980 Excavations at Stoke sub Hamdon Castle, Somerset, 1976 *Proc.SANHS* 124, 61-76.

Leach, P.J. 1984 The priory barn 1977-78, pp.111-24 in Leach (ed) 1984.

Leach, P. (ed) 1984 *The Archaeology of Taunton. Excavations and fieldwork to 1980* (Western Archaeological Trust Excavation Monograph Number 8)

Leach, P. & Dunning, R. 1990 *Ilchester* (Somerset County Council: 31-page illustrated booklet).

Leach, P.J. & Pearson, T. 1984 Benham's garage; excavations 1973-4 & 1978, pp.37-53 in Leach (ed) 1984.

Lean, V.S. 1902 *Collections of proverbs (English & Foreign), folk lore, and superstitions volume 1* (Bristol).

Leech, R.H. 1977 *Romano-British Rural Settlement in South Somerset and North Dorset* (University of Bristol dissertation; copy held in Taunton's local history library).

Leech, R. & Leach, P. 1982 Roman town and countryside 43-450 AD, pp. 62-82 in Aston & Burrow (eds) 1982.

McAvoy, F. 1986 Excavations at Daw's Castle, Watchet, 1982 *Proc.SANHS* 130, 47-60.

McBurney, C.B.M. 1959 Report on the first season's fieldwork on British Upper Palaeolithic cave deposits *Proceedings of the Prehistoric Society* 25, 260-9.

McGarvie, M. 1974 Marston House. A study of its history and architecture *Proc.SANHS* 118, 15-24.

McGarvie, M. 1981 *Witham Friary. Church and parish* (Frome Society for Local Study).

McGarvie, M. 1989 Ponter's Ball *Somerset & Dorset Notes & Queries* 32, 758-9.

Minnitt, S. 1982 Farmers and field monuments 4000-2000 BC, pp. 23-7 in Aston & Burrow (eds) 1982.

Morris, E.L. 1987 Later prehistoric pottery from Ham Hill *Proc.SANHS* 131, 27-47.

National Trust 1987 *Dunster Castle, Somerset* (National Trust guidebook).

Needham, S.P., Cowell, M. & Howard, H. 1988 A technological study of the Ham Hill stone moulds *Proc.SANHS* 132, 15-21.

Norman, C. 1982 Mesolithic hunter-gatherers 9000-4000 BC, pp. 15-21 in Aston & Burrow (eds) 1982.

Page, W. (ed) 1911 *The Victoria History of Somerset.* Volume 2 (reprinted 1969 by The University of London Institute of Historical Research).

Pantin, W.A. 1964 (1962-3) Medieval English town-house plans *Medieval Archaeology 6-7,* 202-39.

Pearson, T. 1984 The keep: H. St. George Gray's excavations, a summary, pp.17-20 in Leach (ed) 1984.

Pevsner, N. 1958a *The Buildings of England. South and west Somerset* (Penguin, London).

Pevsner, N. 1958b *The Buildings of England. North Somerset and Bristol* (Penguin, London).

Phelps, W. 1836 *The History and Antiquities of Somersetshire* Volume I (Priv. print., London)

Pooley, C. 1877 *An Historical and Descriptive Account of the Old Stone Crosses of Somerset* (London).

Pring, J.H. 1880 *The Briton and the Roman on the Site of Taunton* (Taunton).

Rackham, O. 1988 Woods, hedges and forests, pp. 13-31 in Aston (ed) 1988a.

Radford, C.A.R. 1929 The Roman site at Westland, Yeovil *Proc.SANHS* 74, 122-43.

Rahtz, P. 1968 Glastonbury Tor, pp.111-22 in Ashe (ed) 1968.

Rahtz, P. 1979 *The Saxon and Medieval palaces at Cheddar. Excavations 1960-62* (BAR 65).

Rahtz, P. 1982 The Dark Ages 400-700 AD, pp. 99-107 in Aston & Burrow (eds) 1982.

Rahtz, P. & Hirst, S.M. 1987 The chapel of St Columbanus at Cheddar *Proc.SANHS* 131, 157-61.

Read, R.F. 1924 Second report on the excavation of the Mendip barrows *Proc.UBSS* 2 (2), 136-46.

Rigold, S.E. 1957 *Nunney Castle, Somerset* (Dept of the Environment guidebook, HMSO).

Robinson, J.A. 1918 The foundation charter of Witham Charterhouse *Proc.SANHS* 64, 1-28.

Rodwell, W.J. 1984 The keep and adjacent remains: field survey 1977-78, pp.20-6 in Leach (ed) 1984.

Rodwell, W. 1987 *Wells Cathedral. Excavation and discoveries* (The Friends of Wells Cathedral).

Scott Holmes, T. 1911 Religious houses, pp.68-171 in Page (ed) 1911.

Siraut, M.C. 1985 Nettlecombe, pp. 111-20 in Dunning (ed) 1985.

Stanton, W.I. 1981 The Deer Leap stones, Ebbor, Mendip (ST 5179. 4877) *Proc.UBSS* 16 (1), 63-70.

Taylor, C. & Tratman, E.K. 1957 The Priddy Circles. Preliminary report *Proc.UBSS* 8 (1), 7-17.

Taylor, H. 1933 The Tyning's barrow group – second report *Proc.UBSS* 4 (2), 67-127.

Taylor, H. 1951 The Tyning's Farm barrow group third report *Proc.UBSS* 6 (2), 111-73.

Taylor, H.M. & Taylor, J. 1965 *Anglo-Saxon Architecture.* Volume 1 (Cambridge University Press).

Thomas, N. 1976 (2nd ed) *A Guide to Prehistoric England* (Batsford, London).

Thompson, E.M. 1895 *A History of the Somerset Carthusians* (John Hodges, London).

Tratman, E.K. 1959 Maesbury Castle, Somerset *Proc.UBSS* 8 (3), 172-8.

Tratman, E.K. 1966 Decoy mounds on Blackdown, Mendip, Somerset *Proc.UBSS* 11 (1), 44.

Tratman, E.K., Donovan, D.T. & Campbell, J.B. 1971 The Hyaena Den (Wookey Hole), Mendip Hills, Somerset *Proc.UBSS* 12 (3), 245-79.

Vowles, A. 1939 *The History of the Caratacus Stone Winsford Hill* (Minehead).

Waite, V. 1969 (2nd ed) *Portrait of the Quantocks* (Robert Hale, London).

Whitfield, M. 1981 The Medieval fields of southeast Somerset *Proc.SANHS* 125, 17-29.

Wilcox, R. 1980 Excavations at Farleigh Hungerford Castle, Somerset, 1973-76 *Proc.SANHS* 124, 87-109.

Wilson, R.J.A. 1988 (3rd ed) *A Guide to the Roman Remains in Britain* (Constable, London).

Illustration Acknowledgements

Lesley & Roy Adkins: (pages) 2, 8, 10, 12, 13, 21, 22, 25 (bottom right), 28, 30, 36, 39, 40, 42, 43, 45, 46, 47, 48, 49, 51, 52, 54, 55, 57, 58, 60, 61, 63, 64 (top), 65 (top), 66, 67, 68, 69, 71, 73, 74, 75, 79, 81, 82, 84, 86, 88, 89, 90, 92, 93, 95, 97 (left), 99, 100, 103, 106, 107, 109, 111, 112, 114, 115, 116, 119, 120, 121. Mick Aston: 29, 59, 62, 97 (top right). Cambridge University Collection: 20, 91. W. Camden 1607, *Britannia:* 65 (bottom right). Colt Hoare 1824: 31, 123. Haverfield 1911: 38. Knight (ed) 1845: 64 (bottom right). Phelps 1836: 25 (top left), 102. Pooley 1877: 117. Proc. SANHS 9 (1860): 83, 113. Proc. SANHS 11 (1863): 125. Proc. SANHS 36 (1891): 34, 35. Somerset Archaeology and Natural History Society: 32. David Burnett 53, 87, 104, 110.